SELF LOVE

Self-Compassion & Anxiety Workbook:
Learn How You Can Develop Self-
Worth, Inner Strength, Happiness, and
Mindful Living To Eliminate Negative
Self-Talk, Negative Thoughts, Fear, and
Negativity By Loving Yourself First

Dr. Robert G. Neff M.D.

Dr. Kristin K. Germer

David A. Wallace

Table of Contents

PART 1

Chapter 1: Anxiety: The Monster Within

"I know what it's like to be afraid of your own mind."

- Dr. Reid from Criminal Minds
- Obsessing over small worries that constantly distract you
- Whirling from action to action to try to quiet your minds' nagging
- Attempting to drown out anxious thoughts in any way possible, solemnly wishing they would just disappear

If you are here with us today, you are likely living through all the above and more, trying strategy after strategy to eliminate these causes of stress. Or, perhaps you are seeking help for a loved one that has anxiety that is weighing them down. Or, maybe you are simply here to feed your curiosity of what anxiety is and how it plagues the mind. No matter, I work with anxiety every day and have spent the majority of my existence on Earth immersed in it.

My grandfather was such a worrier that he physically shook, *constantly*. His body would tremble from the overwhelming magnitude of worry that lurked within him. He was a burly southern man who favored anything outdoors and fishing. His long, curly locks framed his rounded face with an always generous smile. When he was at his warmest, he was a magnet to others. However, his most natural state was when he was in worry mode.

What did he worry about? Anything and everything. He was worried about all the typical things that grandparents do; along with I'm sure many countless unspoken things.

"Do you have enough to eat?"

"Do you need the salt or pepper?"

"Are you comfortable? Too hot? Too cold?"

Even though he was a burly man, his voice was soft, so anyone listening had to lean in. I think he like the intimacy it afforded. Whenever we were all at ease, he was at ease.

Us grandkids always ran with the joke, *"Grampy, can we pass you the salt and pepper?"* His anxiousness would disappear with a smile and flush of embarrassment. We did this to show our appreciation, to relieve the tension and let him know he was never a burden and that we loved our big burly gramps for who he was.

Our gramps was a people-person, always curious and invested in others. I have very clear memories of coming home and hearing his low but small voice in the answering machine, *"Hello, it is just me again. Just checking in to see how you are coming along…"*

He needed that regular assurance that everything was, in fact, alright and always preferred to hear it firsthand. And if he could do things for someone, that was even better.

As Gramps aged, his anxiety escalated and he became less able to use it in a constructive manner. There were less and fewer ways for him to release his anxious feelings, to the point he became crippled with worried on a daily basis.

When I search into where my own anxiety stemmed from, a picture of Grampy always pops into my mind. When I studied anxiety in graduate school, his shaking body was a perfect analogy. The more time I spent exposed to the study of anxiety in the human body, I began to understand my grandfather better than he likely understood himself most days. I also realized how persuasive anxiety was throughout our family's history. It was what set the foundation for me to deeply understand how much anxiety affected emotions and behaviors.

Thankfully, no one else in my family shook as much as my grandfather did from anxiety; however, looking back, anxiety was the hub of all the spectrum of extremes my family endured. My mother was motivated by her anxiety, while my father was like a balloon, letting stress and anxious feelings build up until he popped with rage.

While no one in my immediate family was ever diagnosed with an anxiety disorder, I can still imagine that just like so many others, they would have felt the same shameful stigma that comes along with all mental health problems, thinking that something is wrong with them. They were simply noticing things in their lives and felt deeply about them; they just didn't have the tools and knowledge to cope with the overload of information.

Through my years as a psychologist, I have gained a different perspective on anxiety and how it alters thoughts and feelings. I have come to see anxiety as a resource and seek to embrace its value in our everyday lives.

Anxiety derives from the feeling of realizing that something we genuinely care about may be at risk, as well as the arrival of resources that we need in order to protect it. Anxiety prompts us to look closer · and pay better attention to messages we receive and helps us to gain the motivation we need to take control of situations. The key to getting back a life driven by anxiety and fear is to take control. This is where I have used my knowledge to help others, in ultimately steering them in a different direction of gaining back their willpower.

How Anxiety Overshadows Everyday Lives

Living in denial, second-guessing your every move, thinking ill thoughts about your future, living in fear of the unknown; all these things can overshadow a person's life and lead to constant anxiety.

If you or a loved one is plagued by anxiety, you have probably endured panic attacks and constant negative nagging in your head on a regular basis or have a phobia of some kind feel ashamed of their "sickness."

Anxiety has the power to make everyday folks feel insane, even though they truly aren't. Just like with all people, some days are better than others, but those who experience symptoms caused by these mental ailments typically have a higher count of bad than good days.

They often feel that they are always under a dark cloud that pours rain, but that rain is not made up of just water. Those drops from the sky above their head are created from startling visions, disturbing logic, feelings of worthlessness and/or hopelessness and looks that they receive from both loved ones and strangers when they truly believe they are in a type of personal crisis or feel as if they are about to be pushed over the edge. This is just a small portion of what it is like to live with anxiety.

What is Anxiety?

Anxiety, in its simplest form, is a bodily reaction to unfamiliar or dangerous environments and scenarios. Everyone has the tendency to get anxious from time to time and feel distressed or uneasy. This happens perhaps before a big game, performing in front of an audience or right before a huge job interview. Feeling anxious is a natural response that our bodies can feel during moments like these. Anxiety gives us the boost we need to be consciously aware and alert to prepare us for certain situations.

Our body's "fight-or-flight" response is under this umbrella of reactions. But imagine feeling like this *all* the time, even during the calmest of moments?

Picture a life where you have issues concentrating on everyday tasks, where you may be frightened to leave the safety of your home when you cannot fall or stay asleep because your mind is in a constant whirlwind of thought? Living with an anxiety disorder is debilitating. That is putting it lightly in some cases.

Causes of Anxiety

Every one of us is unique, which means even common disorders, like anxiety and depression, resonate within each of us differently, as well as why we are living with anxiety, to begin with.

There are several key factors that cause anxiety disorders to grow in the mind:

- Chemistry of the brain
- Environmental factors
- Genetics
- How we grew up
- Life events

The factors listed above are the basics that lay the groundwork to potentially be a victim of anxiety, but those below mixed with any of those above could set one up to be someone that is at a higher risk than others in the development of an anxiety disorder:

- Alcohol, prescription medication or drug abuse
- Chemical imbalances in the body and/or brain
- History of anxiety that runs in family bloodlines
- Occurrence of other mental health issues
- Physical, emotional or mental trauma
- Side effects one has on particular medications
- Stress that lasts an extended amount of time

The feelings and thoughts that anxiety promotes within a sufferer create a bubble that creates lonely thoughts and feelings, which is why it is no surprise that anxiety disorders are the most common of mental illnesses with the U.S, with **over 40 million American adults** living with one of these disorders as we speak.

If it is any consolation, you are by no means alone when it comes to feeling the way you do. There is still a lot of research being put into finding out why anxiety plagues so many individuals, its specific causes and why it resonates within individuals in such vast ways.

Signs & Symptoms of Anxiety Disorders

All of us will experience anxiety in our lives; it is a normal response to stressful life events. But as you have learned so far or experienced for yourself, these symptoms can become much larger than the events of stress them and can interfere heavily with a happy, healthy way of life.

Below are the most common symptoms of anxiety:

- **Worrying** that is disproportionate to the events that trigger it and is intrusive, making it challenging to concentrate on everyday tasks.
- **Agitation** that causes fast heartrates, sweaty hands, dry mouth, etc.
- **Restlessness** or feeling on edge with a constant uncomfortable urge to move that won't go away.
- Becoming **easily fatigued**, either in general or after a panic attack.

- **Difficulty focusing** on everyday tasks.

- **Issues retaining short-term memory** which results in a lack of performance in multiple areas of life.

- Becoming **easily irritable** in the day to day life.

- Constantly having **tense muscles** that may even heighten anxious feelings.

- **Issues falling and staying asleep** due to continued disturbances in the sleep cycle.

- **Panic attacks** that produce overwhelming sensations of fear.

- **Avoidance of social situations** due to a fear of being judged, humiliated, or embarrassed.

- **Extreme fears** about very specific situations or objects that are severe enough to interfere with normal functioning.

Understanding Social Anxiety

Imagine at random times, feeling so uncomfortable in particular situations to the point of not being able to process what is happening around you or difficulty breathing. Welcome to the life of those that deal with social anxiety.

Social anxiety is classified by a major discomfort with social interactions as well as a fear of judgment. There are more than 15 million Americans that deal with this in their everyday lives that struggle with the awkwardness of social settings.

Symptoms of Social Anxiety

The main symptoms of this form of anxiety are feeling intensely anxious when in social situations or avoiding them altogether. Many sufferers have a constant feeling that 'something just isn't right', but are never able to pinpoint it.

As you can imagine, these people have a twisted way of thinking that includes false beliefs of situations and negative opinions from others. Many people fear the interaction days or weeks before the event, which means that social anxiety can manifest in other physical symptoms, such as:

- Sweating
- Shaking
- Diarrhea
- Upset stomach
- Muscle tension
- Blushing
- Confusion
- Pounding of heart
- Panic attacks

The key aspect of social anxiety to remember is that even though these folks have a fear of speaking or interacting with others, it doesn't mean they have nothing to say.

Below are things that those who suffer from social anxiety would say to others to help them understand how they feel:

"I do not want this and I cannot help it. It is not just a bit of nervousness that comes and goes. It is constant stress and living in a world that you start to not recognize."

"In my ability to speak right, I lack confidence. There are many times I want to say something, but hold back because I am afraid of how dumb it may sound or that I will be misunderstood. I am afraid of speaking in groups, phone calls, and approaching people the most."

"I am terrified of people's reactions when I do scrounge up the courage to finally speak."

"My anxiety socially is not a constant. There are certain situations that cause me more anxiety than others. It is a fluid disease."

"Many times, people don't realize that those with this anxiety disorder are suffering because of the lack of physical symptoms. Just because you cannot tell there is something wrong, doesn't mean there isn't."

"I cannot help how ridiculous it may seem."

"It hurts to know that people take my anxiety personally instead of just helping me out."

"I wish I had a social life, but my anxiety won't let me; I am not anti-social."

"It may look like I am zoning out from time to time, but I am actually practicing positive self-talk and breathing techniques to stay calm and ward off a panic attack."

"I am not trying to be standoffish, rude, or snobby, even though it may seem that way when I refuse hugs or don't wish to speak. I simply get overwhelmed and overstimulated easily. All I ask for is respect."

"I want people to break the ice and speak to me first. I am genuinely a nice person, I just have a fear I am unable to control."

"I wish more people understood that when I say I cannot come, it is because the situation I was invited to feels 'impossible', not because I don't feel like it."

"When I leave early, I am not being disrespectful. I just need to fight off a meltdown with some alone time."

"Social anxiety is not 'shyness'; that is like comparing a stab wound to a paper cut."

No one experiences social anxiety in the same way. Each day is like living a life of constant fear; worrying about the disapproval of others, rejection, not fitting in, etc. They are bound to be anxious to enter or begin a conversation.

Chapter 2: Acknowledging Your Anxiety

While the numbers of those that suffer from anxiety in the United States alone exceed 40 million, you may feel alone in your symptoms as well as what triggers them. Things that set off those anxious thoughts and feelings are a bit different for everyone who experiences anxiety. It is important to take time to focus on yourself and learn what things provide you with peace or create tension in your life.

Common Anxiety Triggers

- The hustle and bustle of everyday life. Life is always busy and there never seems to be time to slow down.
- The inevitable fact that we are only growing older.
- Driving, especially on freeways with many cars or across bridges.
- Not living up to the expectations that we set for ourselves.
- The sense of uncertainty. When we are not on control of situations we tend to freak out a bit. This comes from a lack of communication and anxiety making conclusions for us.
- Ambulance, fire or police sirens.
- Stresses at work – Not performing well enough, not having enough time during the course of the workday to get things done, etc.
- Simply thinking about what triggers your anxiety can be a cause for anxiousness in itself.
- Being too hot is often times directly associated with being claustrophobic.

- The inevitable part of life known as death. This especially goes for individuals who have experienced much loss in their lives.

- Being alone.

- The possibility of finding out that people do not like you as much as you think they do.

- Being judged or verbally attacked.

- Large crowds.

- The inability to predict the future. Those with anxiety often dislike surprises.

- Trying new things.

- Being far away from home or other places familiar to you.

- When many people speak to or at you all at once.

- The struggles that your children may face at school.

- Money! This is a big one. Whether it is saving for a big event such as a wedding or purchasing a home or car, the process of paying monthly bills while still trying to save money for other things.

Getting to the Root Causes of Your Anxiety

What many of us do not realize is that many causes that trigger our anxieties to flare up are actually self-produced. While you can blame your situation, family, friends, etc. for you distress, you are the one who perceives life as it goes on around you. The way you view it, analyze and take it all is all dependent on you. The root reasons behind the curtains of 'Play Anxiety' are usually caused by one of the following reasons.

Negative Self-Talk

It is said by research conducted by behavioral specialists that upwards of 77% of all the things we think to ourselves is quite counterproductive and negative. What we don't realize is that we are being our own worst critic and a detriment to ourselves. Learn to become consciously aware of the way you speak to yourself.

Write down any sort of negative thoughts for a day and then each day forward practice transforming those negative words or thoughts into a happy, loving one towards yourself. While it may feel weird at first, it will become second nature to you once you practice it for a while. Your self-talk is just as important of a daily habit as any other.

Unrealistic Expectations

Sometimes we simply just have too high of expectations that create a high world that we struggle to reach. Expecting those to be perfect and remember all the details about you is just ridiculous. If your expectations fly way above you, you are more than likely missing out on grand opportunities and are unable to truly recognize the good things that are happening that you should be celebrating.

This goes for the expectations you have for yourself as well. Are they actually realistic? If not, how can you go about making them more reasonable and achievable?

The "Should" Thoughts

Do you find your brain thinking that you "should do this" and you "should do that" often? Have you ever just taken a moment to actually find the reasoning behind why you "should"? Telling yourself that you should is equivalent to telling yourself that you are not good enough. It leads to negative self-talk fast and should be avoided. Make a positive list of the things you should do or become. Are they yours or someone else's expectations?

Taking Things Too Personally

Those with anxiety feel like many things that occur are actually their fault when in reality they more than likely had nothing to do with someone's disgruntled behavior or a glare they received. Learn to not take things too personally because you never know what may be happening in the life of other people.

"We are all in the same game, just different levels. Dealing with the same hell, just at different devils." If you think you are the cause of someone's actions, speak up and ask instead of just assuming. This will get rid of a lot of assumptions that go into negatively feeding your anxiety.

Our minds are wired to believe the things that we tell it the most. If we are always engaging in negative self-talk, expect too much of others or ourselves, do things we just merely think we "should" do or worry about those around you, your brain will act negatively as well. It is all about building a positive foundation for your frame of mind for all those thoughts of yours to dwell in.

In order to unlock the door to happiness and less stress and/or anxiety, it is time to get thinking in a happy manner!

Pinpointing Your Anxiety

While you can take all the time in the world to read information in regards to relieving anxiety via the internet, books or other media, unless you take action and decide that you truly want to make a change to lower your anxiousness, it will never happen. I am an anxiety sufferer and back just a couple years ago it engulfed my everyday life and drowned me more than a few times.

I finally over time came up with a process that assisted me greatly with determining what triggered my anxious thoughts so that I could get a grip on my life and yield them from continuously taking over my personal life.

- *Stop* – When those feeling of anxiousness begin to hit you, stop and take a moment to make a mental note of what you are doing right at that moment. This is easier said than done, for you might be in the middle of a task, conversation, etc. But it is beneficial to take just a moment to identify when you began to feel anxious.
- *Identify* – Recognizing the onset of anxiety will help you come to the conclusion of what actually causes it for you personally. If you develop the capability to notice triggers and feelings when they start to dwell, you can put a stop to them faster. Many people don't realize they are feeling anxious until their symptoms are outrageously taking over them. Over time, you will be able to catch on more quickly what is threatening your happiness and overall well-being.

- **Write** – As you become an expert of taking moments to make mental notes of why you feel anxious, I find that at the end of the day I write down the events during my day, both the goods one and those that triggered my anxiety. I keep a notepad on my cellular device so that I am quickly able to access it to jot down notes at the moment and then write them down on paper before heading to bed. Be sure to write down as many details as possible – what you are thinking, experiencing and feeling, etc.

- **Analyze** – At the end of the week is when I choose to review what I have written in my anxiety notebook. You can review it at the end of each day, week or month, but I do not recommend waiting any longer than that. I wait at least a couple days to a week so that I can see the pattern that my thoughts made. When you are aware of these patterns you are better able to focus on the causes of anxiety and avoid them.

- **Possibilities** – There are numerous things that you can make the scapegoat when it comes to feeling anxious. If you have adequate knowledge of these ideas, you can review patterns and conquer anxiety. Anxiety in many cases is situational. If you are anxious being in unfamiliar surroundings, expose yourself to these types of circumstances a little time. If your causes are more based on the way you think and view the world, learn to engage in positive self-talk. Once you have a pattern written out, you will be less anxious just by the fact that you have some idea and control over your anxiety situation overall.

SELF LOVE

Chapter 3: Trauma and Anxiety

The journey of life is exciting, scary, ridiculous, confusing and worth it all at once. But there are times that we all go through some type of emotional distress, whether it be mere sadness, rapid anxiety, addictions to outside influences, obsessions with things or people, compulsions we have a hard time controlling, behaviors that are self-sabotaging, physical injuries, anger, and bleak moods, among the hundreds of other things we go through, think and/or feel.

It is important to learn ways to cope when it comes to hard times, no matter the time frame. Something psychologically downgrading can happen in a matter of mere moments and leave you scarred for the rest of your life. Some people seek out help from other individuals who are professionals at understanding the human mind, but others wish to find help within them. Having the knowledge to help yourself is not an easy feat. It may be easy to read pages upon pages of books and self-help websites that provide information, but it is much harder to put those words into actions.

The world is a much different place now than it was just a decade or two ago. Technology has advanced so rapidly that some of us are overwhelmed with it all, especially the consequences that we receive, whether from our own actions or that of another being who acted upon a current mood. Human beings are not the robots that we seem to want to create so badly these days. We are emotionally driven individuals with a lack of having the knack to help ourselves in times of need and/or trouble.

The worst thing about the constant rise of this distress is the fact that there is no one age group or certain targeted individuals that are more likely to go through it. It is happening clear from late grade school levels all the ways into senior living years. Students have much more stress with perpetual levels of testing and pressure to be better. Employees live their hard-earned careers always fighting to make their way up the ladder with not much reward. Older individuals are continuously having their wages and retirement that they worked their entire lives for whisked away.

It is a dog eat dog world out there with a lot of room to make mistakes that can cause even more friction in our personal lives. With the constant pressure to be better than the next, our society has taught us maybe how to be more proficient in terms of getting things done at school or work, but many of us have forgotten the person that is truly important: OURSELVES. If we do not take care of our emotional health, detrimental things can occur. Below are some signs that you may be experiencing emotional distress. Some of the symptoms may surprise you.

Childhood Trauma and Sensitivity to Anxiety

Trauma during childhood can impact our entire lives. According to the Journal of Affective Disorders, children who experience traumatic situations are much more likely to have anxiety and depressions and fall victim to alcohol and drug abuse. The same study found that females are more susceptible than males to develop anxiety, even with the same rates of trauma.

If left untreated, trauma during childhood can have effects that last throughout someone's entire life. They are likely to developmental disorders that branch out to much more than just anxiety as well.

Common Anxiety Disorders Caused by Trauma

Common anxiety disorders that are caused by traumatic events are:

- Panic disorder

- Obsessive Compulsive Disorder (OCD)

- Post-Traumatic Stress Disorder (PTSD)

- Body Dysmorphic Disorder

- Agoraphobia

- Social Phobia(s)

As you can imagine, trauma anytime throughout your life can play a major part in the development of anxiety and other mental disorders in your-lifetime.

Chapter 4: Grabbing your life back from anxiety

Now that you have acknowledged that life could be better and have learned how to interpret why you live a life filled with anxiety, it is time to take your life back, pronto! There is a variety of methods we will discuss in this chapter that can help you gain back the confidence you need to live life to the fullest.

Managing Your Emotions

Emotions are a natural human phenomenon. , and are very present in pressing and painful times. Every day we are driven by some force of emotions:

- We take chances because we get excited about new opportunities

- We cry because we are hurting and make sacrifices for those we love

Those are just a couple examples of emotions; they dictate our actions, intentions, and thoughts with authority to our rational minds. Emotions can become a real problem, however, when we act too fast or we act on wrong types of emotions, which cause us to make rash decisions.

Negative emotions, such as bitterness, envy, or rage, are the ones that tend to spiral out of control the most, especially when triggered. It only takes one slip of our emotions to totally screw up the relationships in our lives.

If you have issues controlling your emotions, here are some steps that you can implement into your everyday life that will help you regain rationality, no matter what challenging situation you are facing:

Don't react right away

You are more likely to make mistakes when you react right away to emotional triggers. When reacting right away to these triggers, you are likely to say and do things that you will later regret.

Before acting on emotions, take a deep breath to stabilize your impulses. Breathe deeply for just a couple minutes and you will be able to feel your heart rate return to normal. One you become calmer, remind yourself that feeling this way is just temporary.

Find healthy outlets

Once you have managed your emotions, you need to learn how to release that build up in the healthiest way possible; emotions are something that you should never let bottle up. Talk to someone you trust. Hearing their opinion of the matter can help to broaden your thoughts and regain control.

Many people keep a journal to write down how they feel. Others engage in exercise to discharge their emotions. Others meditate in order to return to their tranquil state. Whatever activity suits you, find it and use it when emotions get high.

Look at the bigger picture

All happenings in our, both bad and good, serves a purpose in our lives. Being able to see past the moment strengthens your wisdom. You may not understand certain circumstances right away, but over time, you will see the bigger picture as the pieces of the puzzle fall into order. Even when in an emotionally upsetting time, trust that there is a reason that you will comprehend in time.

Replace your thoughts

Negatively fueled emotions create negative recurring thoughts that create cycles of negative patterns over time. When confronted with these emotions, force them out of your mind and replace them with more positive thoughts. Visualize the ideal ending playing out or think about someone or something that makes you happy.

Forgive your triggers

Triggers could be the ones you love the most; you're best friend(s), your family, yourself, etc. There will be times that you may feel a sudden wave of rage when people do things that annoy you or a self-loathing feeling when you remember back to the past when you could have done thing differently. The key to managing your emotions is to first, forgive. This allows you to detach from your jealousy, fury, and resentment. As you forgive, you will discover that disassociating yourself from these feelings will do you the best.

Every day we are constantly reminded of how strong and prominent our emotions are and the power they have. We are bound to take the wrong action from time to time and feel the wrong things. To avoid acting out, simply take a few steps back and calm your spirit that is heightened from outside forces. You will be grateful for mastering your emotions when it comes to building and strengthening meaningful relationships.

Using the Power of Mini Habits

Just after Christmas in the days ending 2016, I was reflecting on the year. I realized that I had tons of room to improve but always failed at keeping up with my New Year's resolutions. Instead, I decided that in 2017, I would explore other options.

On the 28th of December, I made the choice that I wanted to get back in shape. Previously, I hardly if ever exercised and had a consistent guilt about it. My goal was a 30-minute workout, realistic, right?

I found myself unmotivated, tired, and the guilt made me feel worthless. It wasn't until a few days later that I came across a small blog article about thinking the opposite of the ideas you are stuck on. The clear opposite of my 30-minute workout goal was chilling on the couch, stuffing my face with junk food, but my brain went to the idea of 'size.'

What if, instead of carrying that guilty feeling around all the time, I just performed one push-up? I know, right? How absurd of me to think that a single push-up would do anything to help me towards my goal.

What I found was a magical secret to unlocking my potential…when I found myself struggling with my bigger goals; I gave in and did a push-up. Since I was already down on the floor, I did a few more. Once I performed a few, my muscles felt warmed up and I decided to attempt a pull-up. As you can imagine, I did several more. And soon, I exercised for entire 30-minutes!

What Are Mini Habits?

Mini habits are just like they sound; you choose a habit you want to change and you shrink them down to stupidly small tasks.

For instance, if you want to start writing at least 1,000 words per day:

- Write 50 words per day

- Read two pages of a book per day

Easy, right? I could accomplish this in 10 to 20 minutes or so. You will find that once you start meeting this daily requirement, you will far exceed them faster than you would imagine.

What is More Essential than Your Habits?

You might be wondering how you can become more comfortable in your skin and be yourself in a cruel world with these so-called mini habits. Well, think about it; what is more important than the things you do each and every day? NOTHING. Habits are responsible for 45% of how we behave, making up the foundation of who we are and how happy we are in life.

The main reason people fail to change anything in their life, even the aspects they know need to change is because they never instill new habits. Why? Simply because in the past, they have tried to do way too much, all at once. If establishing a new habit requires you to have more willpower than you can muster, you are bound to be unsuccessful. If a habit requires less willpower, you are much more likely to succeed!

Benefits of Mini Habits

There are many additional benefits that come with utilizing mini habits in your everyday life. Here are a few:

- Consistent success breeds more success

- No more guilt

- Stronger productivity

- Formation of more positively impactful habits

- Generation of motivation

Chapter 5: Belittle anxiety with personal empowerment

Having a negative attitude towards life keeps us from being happy and impacts those that we interact daily with. Science has more than enough proof to show how being positive impacts your levels of happiness and terms of success. This is why making positivity a habit with the help of small changes can help you to drastically change your overall life and the mindset you have towards the world.

The life you are living is a direct reflection of your overall attitude. It can be quite easy, almost too easy, to be cynical at the world and see it as a mess of injustice and tragedy, especially thanks to the media that we all spend many hours a day on.

Negativity is holding you back from really enjoying your life and has a great impact on your environment as well. The energy that people bring to the table, including you, is very contagious. One of the best things you can do in your life that is free of charge and simplistic is to offer your positive attitude. This is especially beneficial in a world that loves and craves negativity.

One of my favorite quotes of all time comes directly from the King of Pop, Michael Jackson: "If you want to make the world a better place, take a look at yourself and make a change."

As humans, we are creatures of habit. In this chapter, we will outline small but significant changes that can be made to form positive habits that can drastically change the overall mindset of your life around.

Smile

When asked who we think about most of the time, the most honest answer would probably have to be ourselves, right? This is natural, so don't feel guilty! It is good to hold ourselves accountable and take responsibility for ourselves. But I want to challenge you to put yourself aside for at least one moment per day (I recommend striving for more) and make another person smile.

Think about making someone else happy and that warm feeling you get when you receive happiness. We don't realize how intense the impact of making someone smile can have on those around us. Plus, smiling costs nothing and positively works your facial muscles!

Focus on solutions, not problems

Embracing positivity doesn't mean you need to avoid issues, but rather it is learning how to reconstruct the way you criticize. Those that are positive create criticisms with the idea to improve something. If you are just going to point out the issues with people and in situations, then you should learn to place that effort instead into suggesting possible solutions. You will find that pointing out solutions makes everyone feel more positive than pointing out flaws.

Notice the rise, not just the downfall

Many of us are negative just by the simple fact that we dwell too much on the hate and violence that is in our daily media. But what we fail to notice is those that are rising up, showing compassion, and giving love to others. Those are the stories you should engulf yourself in. When you able to find modern-day heroes in everyday life, you naturally feel more hopeful, even in tough times.

Just breathe

Our emotions are connected to the way we breathe. Think about a time that you held your breath when you were in deep concentration or when you are upset or anxious. Our breath is dependent on how we feel, which means it also has the power to change our emotions too!

Fend off other's negativity

I'm sure you have gone to work cheerful and excited to take on the day ahead, but then your co-worker ruins that happy-go-lucky mood of yours with their complaints about every little thing, from the weather to other employees, to their weekend, etc.

It is natural to find yourself agreeing to what others are saying, especially if you like to avoid conflict. But you are initially allowing yourself to drown in their pool of negative emotions. Don't fall into this trap.

Conflict may arise, but I challenge you to not validate the complaints of a friend, family member, or co-worker next time they are going about on a complaint-spree. They are less likely to be negative in the future if they have fewer people to complain to.

Switch the *"I have to"* mindset with *"I get to"*

I am sure you often fail to notice how many times we tell ourselves that we have to go and do something.

- "I have to go to work."

- "I have to go to the store."

- "I have to pay rent."

- "I have to mow the lawn."

You get the picture. But watch what happens when you swap the word have with the word get.

- "I get to go to work."

- "I get to go to the store."

- "I get to pay rent."

- "I get to mow the lawn."

See the change in attitude there? It goes from needing to fulfill those obligations to be grateful that you have those things to do in your life. This means:

- You have a job to go to

- You have enough money to support yourself and your family to provide a healthy meal

- You have a roof over your head

- You have a nice yard

When you make this simple change, you will begin to feel the warmth of happiness snuggle you like the cold blanket of stress falls away.

Describe your life positively

The choice of vocabulary we use has much more power over our lives than we realize. How you discuss your life is essential to harnessing positivity since your mind hears what you spew out loud.

When you describe your life as boring, busy, chaotic, and/or mundane, this is exactly how you will continue to perceive it and it will directly affect both your mental and physical health.

Instead, if you describe your life as involved, lively, familiar, simple, etc., you will begin to see changes in your overall perspective and you will find more joy in the way you choose to mold your entire life.

Master rejection

You will need to learn to become good at being rejected. The fact of the matter is, rejection is a skill. Instead of viewing failed interviews and broken hearts as failures, see them as opportunities for practice to ensure you are ready for what is to come next. Even if you try to avoid it, rejection is inevitable. Don't allow it to harden you from the inside out.

Rethink challenges

Stop picturing your life being scattered with dead-end signs and view all your failings as opportunities to re-direct. There are little to no things in life that we have 100-percent control over. When you let uncontrollable experiences take over your life, you will literally turn into mush.

What you can control is the amount of effort you put into things without an ounce of regret doing them! When you are able to have fun taking on challenges, you are embracing adventure and the unknown, which allows you much more room to grow, learn and win in the future.

Write in a gratitude journal

There are bound to be days where just one situation can derail the entire day, whether it be an interaction that is not so pleasant or something that happens the night before the day ahead, our mind clings to these negative aspects of the day.

I am sure you have read on multiple sites about how keeping a gratitude journal is beneficial. If you are anything like me, I thought this was total rubbish that is until I started doing it. I challenged myself to write down at least five things that I was truly grateful for each and every day. Scientifically, expressing gratitude is linked to happiness and reducing stress.

I challenge you to begin jotting down things you appreciate and are grateful for each day. Even on terrible days, there is something to be blessed about!

Chapter 6: Everyday techniques to fend off anxiety

Despite the toll that anxiety and its symptoms can have on everyday life and fulfillment, in today's world there are many different techniques and methods you can learn to incorporate into your everyday routine that help you to control and possibly even eliminate anxiety from your life. Each section of this chapter will be dedicated to a specific genre of techniques that anyone has the ability to learn!

Visualization and Anxiety

Seeing is believing, which is a key secret to how entrepreneurs and well-known people in society stand out and achieve success and fulfill their dreams. Visualization is the simple use of imagination through mental imagery to help form visions of what we want in our lives and how we can make them a reality.

There are two main kinds of visualization:

- **Pragmatic Visualization** represents a set of days that helps to gain new ideas and interpret what it says/means to them. It helps those understand structures that lie within a set of data.
- **Artistic Visualization** is similar to pragmatic in that it utilizes visuals to convey information but in a different sense. It is used to show people that data is being monitored carefully and shows particular aspects of data that is connected to one another to depict an entire idea.

So, how does learning about these two kinds of visualization help you in your quest to decrease anxiety? Well, visual techniques help to drastically overcome symptoms of anxiety. When the two types are combined, visualization is powerful in obtaining and staying in a calmer state of mind.

When it comes to anxiety, visualization requires one to picture themselves in a safe, peaceful and/or tranquil environment. Anywhere that makes you happier is where you should be imagining yourself during visualization exercises. It does sound pretty funny at first glance, but trust me when I say there is something about being able to transport your mind to somewhere mentally tranquil. Not only will your mind thank you but your body will too, for it becomes much more relaxed and stress-free when performing these practices. Visualization gives people something to distract themselves from the current world that surrounds them.

Why You Should Be Using Visualization

Beyond visualization itself, you can literally view the best of life Beyond visualization itself, you can literally view the best of life from the comfort of your own couch. This chapter will showcase the benefits that come with the dedicated practice of learning and incorporating ways of visualization into your everyday life.

- Improved quality of relationships – The positive outcomes of utilizing visualization doesn't just end within yourself. Since you are developing a better mindset that aids in your views and beliefs, those around you will like and appreciate the more confident, positive you!

- Boosts your mood – When one practices the methods of visualization, they naturally experience a sort of joy that is quite unexplainable to some. Once you finish one of these sessions successfully, you will more than likely feel boastfully happy, calm and relaxed.

- Relieves stress – Practicing the ways of visualization naturally causes one to be able to relax. It has a way of quieting the mind to be able to think happier, more positive thoughts which tone down loads of stress that pile on our shoulders almost on a daily basis.

- Strengthens the immune system – Thanks to all that dialing down of stress and things that fuel stress, your body is better able to fight off sickness which makes you physically better, longer. This also helps in aiding anxiety because you are not constantly worrying about getting ill all the time as well.

- Ability to learn new things quicker – When the mind is in a calmer state, it is able to pick up and grasp new concepts much easier than when it is bogged down with so many negative thoughts and emotions.

- Able to cope with the feeling of nervousness – When you take time out of your day to practice visualization, you are initially settling all those negative feelings that you may have about yourself and what others may think of you as well. This immensely helps individuals who are naturally more nervous combat that feeling, which leaves room to try and experiment with new things and ideas. Imagine yourself in a great looking outfit giving that inevitable speech that is due soon. Then imagine an applauding audience. It is quite the confidence booster!

- Builds stronger concentration skills – Visualization makes room for your mind to do other tasks efficiently by spring cleaning negative thoughts, feelings, emotions, and past experiences. This doesn't mean it is responsible for getting rid of them 100%, but it helps one to be able to cope and bring down those bad levels to make room for productivity.

- Assists in overcoming recurring issues – When the weight of your entire world is upon your shoulders, it is no wonder that we begin to believe that our lives were just made to be a laughing-stalk to some because of how life's unlucky events have left us feeling. This can lead to long-term problems and beliefs. Visualization combats these two things.

- Can give you a spark of inspiration – During your sessions, if your mind always veers to one idea in particular, perhaps it is time to take initiative and proceed with the steps in achieving it! Visualizing doing something can directly inspire you to do as such.

- Makes one more creative – Visualization not only takes concentration but also a truckload of creativity as well. If you are going to picture something in detail and add the other four senses to that visual, you have to really want to mold it into reality. We all have creative bones in our bodies. Visualization just brings them out more, honing that skill and letting it shine.

- No boundaries – As I have mentioned before, when it comes to visualization, practice makes perfect. Just like with any newly acquired skill, one must learn to hone its practice to be able to tweak it when needed and use it to their utmost advantage. With certain visualization techniques, you can literally picture yourself doing something that would otherwise be usually hard to achieve. With those images in mind, you then have a good idea what you must do to actually and realistically accomplish that image you had in your head during a visualization session. This method knows no bounds!

- Method of practice and rehearsal – Believe it or not, visualization can be a way to practice your favorite sport or nail that upcoming work pitch that you have been reciting and memorizing for days. Picturing yourself doing or performing something is just as effective as actually completing the task at hand. Utilizing visualization with real, physical practice can get you to honing that skill or memorizing things much quicker.

- Picture yourself getting stronger and healthier – Sounds unbelievable, but if you are sick, seeing yourself get better will have the result of getting healthier, sooner. Visualization reduces stress and relaxes your mind, which also assists in healing your body of sickness or physical injury as well. This allows your body to function at its full capacity. You would be surprised what our bodies could accomplish in a day's work if we treated them more like the temples they are and should always be. It is safe to say we take our physical presence for granted most days. And it tends to show more often than not!

- Gives us joy – Many people who practice the ways of visualization tend to picture something that brings them happiness. We almost are never quite in the right place or time in our lives to always have what we want and that is okay! But that doesn't mean we shouldn't get the luxury of seeing it for ourselves, right? Picturing a goal or what we want the most from life can bring us quite a load of temporary happiness if one wants to view it that way. Why temporary? If you can picture it, you can eventually and more than likely make it happen in your future, which is why visualization can be a great motivator.

Aspects of Successful Visualization Practices

There are three aspects to successfully become one with visualization:

- **Practice –** Learning the ways of visualization may actually be more stressful and frustrating for beginners because it is not a practice we are naturally keen to perform. Those that start practicing visualization have a false sense of what the experience is supposed to feel like and have false expectations about the outcome. This inhibits the practice from really taking effect. Visualization is something that has to be practiced daily to work for you long-term. If practiced the right way, it will eventually become second nature to you but only if you really dedicate yourself to learning its ways and practicing it every day until you have it down pat.

- **Utilizes ALL the senses** – Visualization doesn't just use your sense of how a certain peaceful place appears to you in your mind. You have to imagine what your safe space smells, tastes sounds and feels like as well. The more detailed you are in regards to your senses, the better visualization you will have and the more relaxed you can potentially become.

- **Actions** – All human beings experience mental barriers that keep them from being happy and the process of practicing and performing visualization is not excluded from this. Even for visualizing experts, bad thoughts from the course of one's day can inhibit one from getting a clear vision of their safe haven. You have to find a way to release and/or transform those bad thoughts and feelings into something that you can tangibly get rid of.

Forms of Visualization for Anxiety

Visualization is a skill that can be utilized to obtain a better life, especially for those that suffer from an anxiety disorder. Now, we will talk about techniques in the visualization world. Although all of these are not for everyone, try them out and see what works for you.

Meditation

Meditation is a superb form of apathetic visualization that can lead to very powerful results. Visualizing through means of meditation is more of an outgrowth than the main focus. When you begin to incorporate meditation sessions into your everyday routine, you will gradually be opening the door to your inner self, which will then lead you to be able to visualize more clearly and easily.

The more experience you have with meditation, the smoother sessions become and the more you get to see and take away from your visions. It is important not to become frustrated with yourself or discouraged from continuing to practice meditation if you are just starting out.

The whole point of meditation is to empty your brain of thoughts and feelings and to let your mind wander to wherever it wants to go. A vital component of meditation is breathing. Learn to focus on how you take in and let out breaths of air. Let your mind veer off to wherever its little heart desires. Once you begin to practice this technique more often, it will become easier and faster to exhaust your mind of concerns or other worries and let other things come in and explore. It will become second nature for you to sit down, relax and get into a clear state of mind so that you can visualize to your contentment.

Meditation makes way for things that you never thought were actually within you. Once you rid your brainwaves of all that noise from the course of your day, thoughts occur at their own pace.

Altered Memory Visualization

This visualization technique targets past memories and learning how to change them to a more positive standpoint. For those with anxiety about things that stem from their past, this is especially helpful in obtaining a brighter state of mind. This technique is one to utilize if you are one that holds on to past anger and resentment from particular situations that you finally want to rid yourself of.

No one can change the past, but you can teach your brain how it views these past scenarios in your mind. Get into a calmed state and visualize the scenario that you wish had a different outcome. Restore things said that were fueled by anger with comments that are controlled and peaceful. This does take some time and you may have to revisit this scene in your head multiple times to nail the outcome that you wish had resulted from the past situation. It is recommended to not do this day upon day in a row, but rather space out revisiting the scene.

Over time, your brain will begin to only recall what YOU have recreated, making a once painful or uncomfortable situation fade away in memory. Try to imagine little cubicle offices in each major section of your brain. In this instance, I like to picture a little office guy that is in charge of just the bad memories. During these sessions, you are instructing him on how to rewrite particular events that have occurred in the past and once they are rewritten the way you once anticipated them to play out, this office dude can start to shred your memories of these occurrences.

Receptive Visualization

This technique is much like viewing a movie inside your head, but you are the director of the scenes within this movie. Get yourself to a quiet space, lie back, get comfortable and close your eyes. Focus on building the scene in which you want to see acted out in your mind.

Once a clear backdrop and scenery is within your mind, place people, noises, smells and sounds within your scene of this movie. It is best to slowly build your way up to the actual scene until you are comfortable and content with it, then it is time for action! Focus on feeling involved within this scene of your "movie."

Treasure Map

This visualization technique not only uses mental fundamentals but also physical components as well. You will need to have an idea of what you want to visualize before getting to the nitty-gritty of performing this method. Start by using your art skills to draw out some type of physical representation of the components you need to achieve in order to reach your ultimate goal.

For example, perhaps you have an upcoming test that you want to get a great grade on. Draw out a building symbolizes a school, a book that you will need to use to study for this test and then a representation of yourself. Try to make your drawing detailed, but do not worry about the maturity of your art abilities too much here. It is not the drawings themselves that are important, but rather what you are imagining WHILE sketching them out.

As you draw out your "map to success", your mind is actually visualizing ways that will get you to where you want to be. Patience is a key with this particular technique, for it does take a bit of time to truly become completely mentally occupied in this exercise. It is crucial to take your notepad and pen to a quiet space and to not be around anything distracting such as a radio, television, people or phones.

How to Design Your Own "Safe Space"

Safe places or spaces are a mind's sanctuary, created for the purpose of retreat if one needs a mental location to be able to visualize or hone their meditative state and reduce stress. Creating one of these is kind of like personalizing a physical space in your home. You want to do anything to truly make it YOURS.

It can be anything from a room inside an imaginary home, a room in your realistic home that you want to visualize differently, the beach, a comforting outdoorsy area, etc. As you meditate or relax and begin to dive deeper into your imagery or visualization session, this is the place you imagine you want to go. It is anywhere that you wish to return to time after time, so put some effort and thought into where you will always find comfort in mentally retreating to.

- **Brainstorm** – The goal is to develop a place that you feel calm, content and happy within, no matter the reason that you retreat to it. If you have difficulty seeking out such a place, start by looking through art, magazines, books, old photographs, etc. Always lean towards ideas that burst with positivity for you.
  - o Are you more apt to feel calmer in an outdoor/natural setting or do you feel better within the walls of some type of structure?
  - o Are there pieces of writing such as within books, poems of stories that make you feel at ease?
  - o Do you feel more comforted by populated areas or tranquil areas?

- **Think of a time where you felt happy and safe** – Memories are the best areas to seek things that bring joy to you. Think back to memories that you were happy, content, playful, peaceful, etc. Write these down in detail. It could be literally anywhere, as long as it brought contentment to you.
  - o Where did this memory occur?
  - o How old were you?
  - o Why did this memory make you happy?
  - o Who was with you within this memory?

- **Create various rooms** – Your safe space does not necessarily have to be just 2D, one room vision. It can have various sections, compartments or rooms within it. This allows you to trek to different areas throughout your visualization sessions. This also allows one the ability to be able to compartmentalize issues and deal with them one part at a time.

- *Fill your space with cherished people* – There are many individuals that would rather be alone while in their safe place, while others prefer the company of their favorite people. Imagine who makes you happy and during the course of a visualization session, imagine greeting them and welcoming them into your safe space. This also goes for people in your life that may have passed away that you miss and wish to see. Having conversations with them and asking for advice could make a world of difference!

- *Utilize ALL your senses* – Seeing is believing, but visions of your safe place are a lot more believable and turn in better results if you learn to engage all your senses while within them. Engulf yourself in tastes, sounds smells and how things feel between your fingers and toes and against your skin. It will enhance your visualization experience ten-fold.

- *Write out all the details* – Once you have taken the dedicated time to develop and build your safe place, write down all the tiniest details that you can remember. Writing in a lot of detail can assist you in returning to that place in your mind easier and more efficiently. Some individuals even videotape, sculpt, draw or paint out their descriptions for safekeeping for future use.

  o Are there animals or people?

  o What do you feel?

  o How small or big is your space?

  o What colors?

  o What surrounds you?

  o What is the ultimate backdrop or setting?

- **Visualize positive results** – The main rule of thumb for visualization is imagining situations acted out in positive manners. This involves a heavy amount of thinking happily and setting up a content scene. Imaging positive outcomes are really just a more in-depth version of regular run-of-the-mill positive thinking.

Developing Anxiety Routines

Anxiety routines are any type of daily routine that you use to calm yourself down in stressful situations and that leaves you feeling physical, mental or emotionally distressed. These routines are meant to help you bounce back from the depths of your own thoughts and live a life full of more passion and fulfillment.

This means it is very crucial to choose routines that not only suit you but are healthy, too. Life runs smoother when you have a routine to fulfill those nasty little voices in your head or when you feel like you may make a bad choice because of your anxiety symptoms. Sadly, some people choose unhealthy habitual routines that not only push them back into a negative state but may even provoke symptoms of anxiety and make them worse.

These bad routines could be anything from drug use, both illegal and prescription, large consumption of alcohol or heavy smoking of cigarettes, etc. You get the picture. Creating an anxiety routine for yourself should not include things that will cause you greater harm in the long run. Honestly, habits like those stated above are only going to make your symptoms worse.

As human beings, we are automatically wired to detect any sort of negative energy that may cause us harm. Anxiety becomes so bad within certain people simply because our bodies do not quite know the difference between stressful triggers that are actually harmless to us versus actual, life-threatening aspects that may be sprung upon us.

Our bodies are made to react to protect ourselves. This is why being mentally prepared for the day that lies ahead of you is so crucial, especially for anxiety sufferers. It is important to back up our thoughts with an extra layer of positivity to promote a sense of safety and well-being. This is much easier said than done, especially when life may not have been a very good friend to you as of late. But being able to mentally develop a positive sense of self is the first step in creating daily routines that help pave your way to a successful life to live and your future.

Routines to Decrease Anxiety

With the right amount of inspiration, the first day or two of adding a new routine to your life can be exciting. You know you are making a positive change that will hopefully help you feel better about yourself and the life you live. However, self-care routines can be a hard thing to manage and utilize on a regular basis once the newness of acting upon it wears off.

Anxiety can leave some sufferers so dismayed by anxious or sad thoughts that they want nothing more than to do away with anything that resonates positive energy. But this is the exact opposite of fighting for yourself and your happiness. Everyone has their bad days and moments and by all means, you are allowed to have and live those. But it is important not to stay tucked away in them for long periods of time.

Developing and executing specific daily routines that you are comfortable with gives those a step by step plan for the day and keeps you prepared for situations or other anxiety triggers from leaping out and mugging you of your happiness. Routines, kind of like exercise, are things we practice daily to keep us in shape, but anxious routines keep our minds in check. You never know when something will catch you off guard, when a person may ask you something that is bothersome or when a debilitating symptom of anxiety will hit you throughout the course of the day. It is better to be prepared than not to be, right?

The Importance of a Balanced Morning Routine

Many functions within routines do them absolutely no good. When the alarm goes off, they tend to hit snooze a few times. When they finally decide to open their eyes, they automatically reach for their phones and look at updates on social media. Many people are already let down by the fact no one messaged them or liked their posts throughout the night.

When their feet finally touch the floor to stand up out of bed, they are already on a path to a negative, self-destructing day. They take a quick shower, down a bowl of cereal and chug a cup of coffee and get to their day job...what is the point?

This lack of routine is non-beneficial. We see our unstructured lives as having no real purpose, which results in a lack of inner peace. We are destroying our happiness without realizing it!

Benefits of a Morning Routine

Creating a morning routine is not only a big part in relieving anxiety, but it also boosts productivity, brings out your inner positivity, helps you to develop and successfully sustain good relationships, as well as being a big reducer of negativities. Morning routines alone have been shown to be the best strategy for reducing stress and relieving those pesky symptoms of anxiety, no matter how long they have resided within you.

Morning routines keep you consciously aware and more grounded throughout the day. In fact, many who were once stubborn and did not want to incorporate a daily routine were eventually surprised at how much better they felt each and every morning. Anxiety levels dropped and confidence and happiness levels substantially rose. A morning routine can literally reduce your anxiety by as much as sixty percent!

Steps to Include in Your Morning Routine

When you wake up earlier, you know that you have plenty of time to get up and get ready for your day, which aids in decreased stress levels. If there is adrenaline pumping throughout your body as you rush around to head out the door, it sticks with you for the rest of the day.

Sounds like a waste of time, but making your bed each morning is a powerful task that helps you gain the momentum you need to get pumped for the day ahead. For those that suffer from anxiety and depression, making the bed is simple but can make a huge difference because you know you have completed one task if not anything else.

Meditation and prayer is a subject with many critics. People view meditation as an act performed only by spiritual individuals. Practicing mindfulness daily has positive side effects that can trigger feel-good hormones in the brains that aid in reducing levels of stress, anxiety and even depression.

Mixing meditation and prayer within your morning routine can be quite vitalizing, giving clarity to your life and your decisions. If you wish to learn more about the power behind the act of prayer, it will be covered in the following chapter The Empowerment of Prayer.

Taking an ice cold shower in the mornings has been proven to provide the human body with a great number of benefits. Cold exposure, also known as cold shower therapy, is nothing new. Our ancestors utilized it as a remedy to treat mental ailments. Showering in cold water provides the body with adequate circulation and tones the skin nicely.

The cold feeling kicks positive responses throughout the body into overdrive. It accelerates the repairing of cells, which reduces inflammation, pain, and speeds up our metabolic processes. The icy waters help lower negative levels that depression and anxiety can hover over us. Standing under the cold water for just a couple minutes can yield you these benefits.

Substitute your breakfast with coffee or tea to bump up energy levels and replace your usual breakfast eats. This is not recommended for absolutely everyone, but if you are trying to find ways to keep hunger away for the first portion of your day, give it a shot!

Learn how to utilize a journal to make "morning pages" as part of your routine in the mornings. This is my personal favorite way to "mind dump" any curious or troubling thoughts you had during the previous day and the night before, as well as random ideas that pop into your mind. I write in my journal after taking a shower, since great ideas tend to spring during those few minutes. When you are able to write down all the negative feelings on paper, you can then get through the day with a clearer state of mind.

Practice gratitude by jotting down things you would miss if they were no longer in your life, such as objects, people, etc. into your morning pages.

To start the day on a positive note, jot down what you are looking forward to that day. This tells our brains to look up, think up and be bright and helps to relieve anxiety.

Write down your intentions at the beginning of each day, no matter how corny they may sound, such as "I will choose to be consciously present today."

Write out important tasks that you wish to achieve during the day to ensure you will feel prepared and have a fulfilling plan. This will ease your mind so that you can develop a clear path of action to achieving that days' goals.

I know I have mentioned writing a lot, but like I said before it is a powerful tool. Every morning our brains are ready to go and on high alert, so it is good to have a well-thought-out plan of action.

Write down at least three to five of the most important tasks that you have to complete. Focus on ones that stress you out just thinking about them. Then, ask yourself the following questions about the tasks you have jotted out so that you can prioritize them accordingly:

When you wake up earlier, you know that you have plenty of time to get up and get ready for your day, which aids in decreased stress levels. If there is adrenaline pumping throughout your body as you rush around to head out the door, it sticks with you for the rest of the day.

Sounds like a waste of time, but making your bed each morning is a powerful task that helps you gain the momentum you need to get pumped for the day ahead. For those that suffer from anxiety and depression, making the bed is simple but can make a huge difference because you know you have completed one task if not anything else.

Meditation and prayer is a subject with many critics. People view meditation as an act performed only by spiritual individuals. Practicing mindfulness daily has positive side effects that can trigger feel-good hormones in the brains that aid in reducing levels of stress, anxiety and even depression.

Mixing meditation and prayer within your morning routine can be quite vitalizing, giving clarity to your life and your decisions. If you wish to learn more about the power behind the act of prayer, it will be covered in the following chapter The Empowerment of Prayer.

Taking an ice cold shower in the mornings has been proven to provide the human body with a great number of benefits. Cold exposure, also known as cold shower therapy, is nothing new. Our ancestors utilized it as a remedy to treat mental ailments. Showering in cold water provides the body with adequate circulation and tones the skin nicely.

The cold feeling kicks positive responses throughout the body into overdrive. It accelerates the repairing of cells, which reduces inflammation, pain, and speeds up our metabolic processes. The icy waters help lower negative levels that depression and anxiety can hover over us. Standing under the cold water for just a couple minutes can yield you these benefits.

Substitute your breakfast with coffee or tea to bump up energy levels and replace your usual breakfast eats. This is not recommended for absolutely everyone, but if you are trying to find ways to keep hunger away for the first portion of your day, give it a shot!

Learn how to utilize a journal to make "morning pages" as part of your routine in the mornings. This is my personal favorite way to "mind dump" any curious or troubling thoughts you had during the previous day and the night before, as well as random ideas that pop into your mind. I write in my journal after taking a shower, since great ideas tend to spring during those few minutes. When you are able to write down all the negative feelings on paper, you can then get through the day with a clearer state of mind.

 Practice gratitude by jotting down things you would miss if they were no longer in your life, such as objects, people, etc. into your morning pages.

To start the day on a positive note, jot down what you are looking forward to that day. This tells our brains to look up, think up and be bright and helps to relieve anxiety.

Write down your intentions at the beginning of each day, no matter how corny they may sound, such as "I will choose to be consciously present today."

Write out important tasks that you wish to achieve during the day to ensure you will feel prepared and have a fulfilling plan. This will ease your mind so that you can develop a clear path of action to achieving that days' goals.

I know I have mentioned writing a lot, but like I said before it is a powerful tool. Every morning our brains are ready to go and on high alert, so it is good to have a well-thought-out plan of action.

Write down at least three to five of the most important tasks that you have to complete. Focus on ones that stress you out just thinking about them. Then, ask yourself the following questions about the tasks you have jotted out so that you can prioritize them accordingly:

- Which tasks will help me inch closer to achieving my main goal?
- What task do I have the most fearful anxious thoughts about?
- Which tasks have the potential to cancel out others if done successfully?

Spend 90 minutes every day working towards accomplishing your priorities. Targeting your main goals during the morning hours help you to get them accomplished productively.

Other Morning Methods to Relieve Anxiety

Play uplifting music to ensure an upbeat, positive mood. Create a playlist to play throughout your morning routine. Make your phone's alarm tone a good song to wake up to. You would be surprised at what a difference this effortless step takes.

Spend time with a pet(s) to help raise your dopamine and serotonin levels, resulting in lessened anxiety and depression. Pets also motivate us to climb out of bed and give us the initiative to take on the day, even when our anxiety tries to get the best of us. Adding them to your morning routine is a bonus for not only you but for your pet's well-being too!

Change your scenery in simple ways; Go outside, take a walk. Visit your favorite café and grab a coffee. Go out with a friend. The longer you dwell in a space that sucks away happiness, the worse you will feel.

Interactions with the outside world can be enough to distract you from your anxious habits. This is another reason routines are so important in aiding anxiety. Avoiding responsibilities can actually damage you mentally more than you realize. It is good to get your attention off the darkness of life that resides inside your head. It only makes your anxiety worse when you sit around and obsess over it.

Coping with anxiety and its symptoms can lead to a life of great discomfort. Having some type of structure in the form of routines can be quite crucial to one's success in living a happy, go-lucky life. The next few chapters will cover other types of routines in detail that can help relieve and maybe even make your symptoms disappear for good! It is all about you to initiate making the change.

Chapter 7: Transforming Your anxiety for a better life

If you are feeling anxious or depressed about your future and are allowing negative thoughts to get the best of you and dampen your motivation for success, then learning to use anxiety to your advantage is a must.

Personally, I have learned to choose to view my anxiety has a valuable asset that yields me to lead a more authentic life. I live empathetically, for my anxiety has made me a vulnerable person and thus, helped me deepen my life's relationships.

Having anxiety just means I am not mellow enough to take things for granted in life, therefore, making life a richer experience all the way around. In fact, there are a few inspirational ways that anxiety has helped me to elevate my life:

- Got me actively involved in personal development
- Taught me how to think in the present and act now
- Got me reading more books and discover how it heals the mind
- Started me on tracking my success and not just on failure
- Taught me how to make a positive game out of my life
- Assisted me to take control over my life
- Reconnected me to the habit of learning new things every day
- Showed me the power of meditation and visualization
- Allowed me to see that I am not the only one in my life that suffers from degrees of anxiety
- Has taught me to be a more actively vulnerable person

Using Anxiety to Your Advantage

Believe it or not, anxiety can be used for good and can be a powerful force in motivating yourself to achieve your desires. Using stress to add momentum to your life is constructive, instead of allowing it to deconstruct our lives.

Redefining danger

You must learn to see anxiety differently; anxiety, before our brains get a hold of it and dwell, is just a warning sign used for our survival. At this point, you are allowing anxiety to make you feel panicked. But even when that warning sign lights up, it doesn't mean you are in danger. You must save this energy for when you really need to make quick decisions.

Create a list of less to most dangerous to help identify a good spectrum of threats. With that comparison, you will be able to see what "dangerous" situations are safe and which ones are frightening.

Channel your stress properly

Diamonds don't grow from trees; they are coals that turn into something more beautiful through pressure. Channeling stress positively into energy for motivation does take time and can be physically and emotionally draining.

But instead of allowing negative thoughts take hold of you and send you down that same spiraling hole of anxiety, look at the situation before you differently; view it as your time to shine! When negativity starts to manifest in your mind, challenge those thoughts. When you challenge them, you will find that the negativity in them is totally empty in the first place.

Stop trying to do your best

There are two kinds of people: those that do their best and those that can do better. However, those that strive to do their best constantly are the ones that end up emotionally drained than those who do better. Why? Because when you do your best, you are settling. When you strive to do better, you accept that you are not doing as good as you know you can. For anxiety sufferers, what they do isn't good enough for them. They either drown in their shortcomings or have learned to take the opportunity to improve themselves.

In those with anxiety, underestimation is a common cognitive distortion. When we tell ourselves that we can do better, we know how to reject our deficiencies and go out of their way to prove themselves wrong.

Chapter 8: Battling anxiety like a true warrior

"The only thing we have to fear is fear itself."

- President Theodore Roosevelt

Marines, SEALs, and Special Forces have no choice but to face life-threatening danger head-on regularly. The fact is, if they do get caught up in fear, they are more likely to lose their lives. While many of us will thankfully never have to face these experiences, why aren't we using the fear-crushing tactics that they use in our own personal lives?

Spend time preparing

If you are worried about a work presentation, stressing over a job interview, or freaking out about the upcoming rap battle that might help you move out of your mom's house, then stop, prepare, and practice instead of sitting around.

The key is to lose yourself in the moment, which you to by devoting a ton of energy into preparing for what you are worried about. Spend 75% preparing and 25% for the actual event.

SEALs are able to erase fear by practicing upcoming mission until they feel naturally confident. When the unknown becomes more known to them, they don't have to lie to themselves about the risks, but instead put themselves in a better position to handle the unknown, which develops confidence.

Learn to manage fear

One of the best ways to deal with fear is to laugh about it. What? You read that right! Laughter lets you know that things are going to be okay and work out. Don't worry; there is evidence to back this theory up. A study by Stanford University showed that those that were trained to make jokes to respond to negative images. This is a much healthier way to deal with fear. The world is an inevitably twisted place, so seeing the funnier side of things makes it easier to deal with.

Breathe

When your heart is beating from your chest, your joints turn into Jell-O, and sweat is pouring off your face, then the best thing you can do to calm the physical manifestations of fear derived from anxiety is to breathe.

That simple? YES. By just inhaling for four seconds and exhaling for four seconds, SEALs can calm their nervous systems and maintain control of their natural biological responses to fear.

You are essentially bending your body's software to better control the hardware. In other words, you are giving yourself a pretty bomb superpower! Breathing helps the body go from the fight-or-flight response of the sympathetic nervous system to the relaxed response of the parasympathetic nervous system.

Tactical breathing used by Navy SEALS for performance just prior to a tense situation or during a workout:

Breathe through the nose. It's very important to breathe through your nose since breathing through the nose stimulates nerve cells that exist behind sternum near the spine that triggers the parasympathetic nervous system. Anxiety is a sympathetic response and parasympathetic counteracts that. This calms your body, which then calms your mind.

1. Relaxed sitting position and right handle on the belly.
2. Activate the breath by pushing belly out and then inhale deeply for a count of four. Inhale to the belly. This pulls breath deep into the lungs. Exhale through the nose for a count of four, pulling the belly button toward the spine. Repeat this three times.
3. Now breathe in through belly and diaphragm for a count of four, again inhaling into your belly and this time lifting your chest. Again, exhale for a count of four so that your rib cage falls and your belly button pulls toward your spine. Repeat three times.
4. Next, use the same technique, this time inhaling for a count of four through the belly, diaphragm and your chest, with a slight raise of shoulders for inhaling. Exhale for a count of four three the chest, diaphragm, and then the belly. Repeat three times, eventually working your breaths up to eight counts.

Next, box breathing is a technique used by the U.S. Navy SEALS to maintain focus and to calm nervous system after a tense situation, such as combat, an intense workout or anytime the desire is to center and focus.

Trains for diaphragmic breathing or deep breathing. Relaxes the whole system and provides oxygen to the brain to focus better. Improves energy. It can also be used by you to regain your sense of balance, concentration, and relaxation and can be practiced at any time. Use the same technique as tactical breathing but you use a five-count hold between breaths.

1. Get in a relaxed sitting position
2. Inhale deeply through the nose for five seconds
3. Hold the air in your lungs for five seconds
4. Exhale for five seconds, releasing all the air from your lungs
5. Hold your lungs empty for five seconds
6. Repeat for five minutes, or as long as you feel necessary

Don't keep things bottled up

Fear is just like terrible liquor; it sucks when you drink it and has negative effects that last a long time, which is why it is important to deal with it before and after the fact.

Talking about scary experiences helps soldiers locate the meaning behind it all. This communication allows them to process what they have been through positively and helps them to create closer relationships with their mates. Scared? Admit it to a friend. Hearing it out loud can help you pull it out, confront it, and deal with it.

Overpower that inner nagging voice

We are all aware of the inner chatter that occurs in our mind on a daily basis. In fact, our inner voice can be really negative the majority of the time. Wouldn't it be cool to have an inner monologue that reminds us how confident and awesome we are? Wouldn't it be great to have an inner motivational speaker to get us through tough times?

Well, you can. In times of stress, our brains are wired to create self-talk that can increase our feelings of fear. As a soldier, they are expected to fight against their inner self-talk and focus on positive portions of experiences. With practice, they are easily able to ignore or even erase the negativity their brains are throwing at them. So, you can do the same in your own life.

Fear and anxiety thrive when we imagine the worst. We developed imagination to be able to project into the future so we can plan ahead. However, a side effect of being able to imagine possible positive futures is being able to imagine things going wrong. A bit of this is useful; after all, there really might be muggers or loan sharks. But uncontrolled imagination is a testing ground for anxiety and fear that can spoil otherwise happy lives.

Some people misuse their imagination chronically and so suffer much more anxiety than those who either future-project their imaginations constructively or who don't tend to think about the future much at all. Anxious, chronic worriers tend to misuse their imaginations to the extent that upcoming events feel like catastrophes waiting to happen. No wonder whole lives can be blighted by fear and anxiety.

Think of the worst-case scenario

No matter what you are afraid of, you always have the opportunity to avoid it for the rest of your life. However, soldiers don't get that choice. They face similar situations time and time again that scare them. To ensure fear doesn't overrule them, they simulate stressful scenarios and try to experience the emotions with them as well.

Instead of thinking happy thoughts and ignoring what you are afraid of, start looking at the worst things that can possibly happen. When you are able to picture the worst fear and stay within an emotional experience instead of pushing yourself out of it, your mind tends to get over the fear naturally.

Reframe your mindset

Reframe you definition of symptoms. Reframe the symptoms of anxiety - give them a different meaning. Those sweaty palms, racing heart, and lightheadedness can mean a panic attack or they can mean the most exciting and fun adventure of your life! Your body doesn't know the difference and it is just doing what it does by nature, but you can choose how you define that sudden rush. Don't believe me?

How do you think those adrenaline junkies dives off cliffs, jump motorcycles or swim with sharks? Their definition of what we call fear is definitely different. They still experience the same potent chemicals coursing through their body, but the sensations have a different meaning to them. What you experience as fear, dread and near death can be defined as thrilling, exciting, and aliveness to someone else.

The beautiful thing about consistently and purposely redefining these symptoms is you can actually rewire your brain. This leads us to neuroplasticity.

Neuroplasticity

Neuroplasticity occurs with changes in behavior, thinking, and emotions. With conscious practice, we can alter our neural pathways to move naturally towards our desired emotions, such as being thankful, calm, and happy and away from anger, stress, and panic.

As you choose to respond with positive emotion, you can strengthen the neural pathways to the desired emotions. As you make more neural connections over time to your desired emotion, the pathways to the negative reactions eventually become weaker and scrambled. This even works while using mental rehearsals of the situation and practicing your desired response.

Remember, this can also work in reverse. If you have a habitual response to circumstances, such as being angry in a traffic jam and you repeat these responses over and over in a high state of emotion, you will strengthen the neural pathways towards the emotion of anger in that situation. The masters over the centuries who taught positive thinking and faith may have actually been on to something and now we can prove it scientifically.

Get moving

Exercise is usually associated with weight loss, improved physical health, and a stronger immune system. But the benefits of exercise can expand much more. Exercise is just as important for your mental fitness as it is your physical health.

Aerobic activity promotes the release of endorphins that are released in the brain and act as painkillers, which also help to increase a sense of well-being. Endorphins also improve energy levels, provide a better night's sleep, elevate your mood and provide anti-anxiety effects. Exercise also takes your mind off of your worries and breaks the cycle of negative thoughts that contribute to anxiety.

It is recommended to perform 30 minutes or more of exercise five days a week to have a significant impact on anxiety symptoms. You don't need a formal exercise program at the gym to experience these benefits. Light physical activity has been shown to have the same effects, including gardening, housework, washing the car and walking around the block. These can be done in small intervals throughout the day.

It's more important to do some sort of physical activity on a consistent basis than to aim for something that is not sustainable. Be realistic and if you need to start with smaller goals, do so. This is all about taking care of yourself in a way that works for you.

The single, most important natural tool you can use to beat anxiety is regular exercise. It sounds cliché, but the truth is that exercise affects the mind and body in ways that science is still discovering.

There is a reason that anxiety prevalence has grown with our increasingly inactive lifestyles. Jogging every day can make a world of difference in how you deal with stress, how your anxiety symptoms manifest, and how you regulate your mood.

The best methods of exercise to combat anxiety are:

- **Running** releases feel-good hormones that have exponential mental health benefits. It can help you fall asleep faster, improve memory, lower stress levels, and protects against developing depression.

- **Hiking** in a wooded or hilly location has natural calming effects on the brain. Being around plants and Earthly sights helps to reduce anxiety thanks to the chemicals plants emit. Plus, being out in nature is great for your health and memory function.

- **Yoga,** a lot like meditation, has been found to significantly reduce anxiety and other neurotic symptoms that can lead to irritability and depression. It not only strengthens your core but helps you to focus on breathing, which is the key to relaxing the mind and combating anxiety.

Chapter 9: Rediscovering yourself after hurricane anxiety

Those that live with and through the darkness of anxiety can find themselves waking up each day unhappy. Life is short and there comes a time where re-evaluating your life in order to revamp parts of it to ensure your happiness and fulfillment.

We all get lost in life from time to time. We forget old passions we had, give up interest in pursuit of something else, etc. But it is never too late to rediscover what makes you great and what makes you feel truly alive.

When were you the happiest?

Take a moment to remember when you were the most content with your life. In high school? College? Before marriage, family, and kids? When you began your family? Started your business? Pursued a new hobby?

No one peaks at the same time or levels in their lives. The key to regaining contentment is not to think of those fond times as "the past", but to figure out how to find that feeling of happiness again where you currently are in your life. How can you re-incorporate those things that brought you joy in the life you are living now?

What makes you unhappy?

What makes your blood pressure shoot through the roof? Figuring out the things that push your last buttons is just as important as knowing what helps you keep a positive outlook. When you are able to clearly point out the toxic influences, you will be better able to erase them and develop better, healthier ways of living.

We tend to hold onto things from the past that has negative impacts on our current lives. What grudges are you holding onto? These are toxic and are keeping you from being your best self! No matter what it is, from a toxic ex-partner to a job that drains you, cutting these negative influences will allow you ample space to grow in a positive direction.

Write!

When negative thoughts are constantly bouncing around the brain, it can be very easy to become overwhelmed. We tend to forget how much our daily thoughts impact our lives. They take hold of our power, telling us who we are and what are and aren't capable of. We are the only ones that have the power to take action to erase pesky thoughts from inhibiting our success in life.

I have found that organizing thoughts by writing them down makes them more abstract. When you can visualize them on paper, it makes them concrete.

Write out a list of pros and cons, random thoughts that pop up, poetry, grocery lists, anything that comes to mind. All writing can be therapeutic and helps us to rediscover how our voice sounds, which radiates who. I challenge to find yourself again with the power of good old pen and paper.

Learning to Love Yourself Again

To rediscover yourself, you need to learn how to love yourself again for who you are, and all parts of yourself, including your flaws and everything you have endured. There are millions of places that offer up 'good advice' to practice self-love, but they never explain exactly how to do so.

Loving yourself is a vital piece of the puzzle when it comes to positive personal growth. It allows us to fulfill our dreams and create happy and healthy relationships with others too.

Care about yourself as much as you care about others

This sounds almost too simple, but many of us are not selfish enough when it comes to fulfilling our wants and needs. It is hard to remember that you are not selfish when it comes to caring about yourself and your wellbeing.

Showing yourself compassion shows those in your life that you are able to take care of yourself. No one can pour from an empty pot, which means you need to take care of yourself in order to take care of others in your life. Treat yourself the way you treat your best friend, with caring, concern, and gentleness, no matter what is happening in your life.

Maintain boundaries

Jot down a list of things you need emotionally, both what is important to you and what upsets you. The list can be made up of anything, from wanting sympathy to being celebrated, to being cared for, etc. Whatever is important to you, no matter how silly it sounds, Write. It. Down.

We can often find ourselves smack dab in the middle of the confusing conflict and wonder how we got there in the first place. We ask ourselves how we attracted this situation and the people in it with us.

While you still need to take responsibility for your actions, it is also crucial to not fall into a pit of self-blame that can cause stress, but rather really look into what is occurring. Many people lack inner confidence and have no idea what they are worth. This lack can leave us living in a sum-zero equation; we are loved completely or become completely unlovable.

I have found from my psychological studies and personal experiences that there are two very simple questions to help anyone restore healthy boundaries in their life to live a dignified life:

What does this situation negatively represent about yourself? How are you tolerating situations and the behaviors of those around you reinforces your low-worth within you? Those in our lives are a mirror of our own biases, hopes, and fears. "All anger stems from anger at the self."

What is your worst fear about saying "no"? Have you ever been left with the thought of you are a bad person because someone's behavior has left you feeling guilty? Well, stop! Challenge that thought by thinking about other situations you have been through. When that happens, the thought that you are a "bad person" falls apart. What matters, in the end, is simple math: people will either add or subtract to your life.

So, what have you written? The things you write are what you should consider your personal boundaries. When someone ignores something on that list, you should consider it as them crossing boundaries that you have respectively set for yourself. Do not ignore how you feel if this happens, for they are there to tell you what is right from wrong.

Inform others about the boundaries you have set for yourself and be forthcoming with what you will and will not tolerate. When you are assertive with your boundaries, this plays an important part in building a positive self-esteem and allows you many opportunities to reinforce your beliefs, what you cherish, and what you deserve from life.

Do YOU?

Take the time for yourself to establish the things that make you feel good about yourself and about your life as a whole, no matter what it is. Just learn to be aware of how you feel when you go about acting on certain things. For example:

- Are you exhausted by the work you do, but feel thrilled when gardening?
- Are you joyful when reading out loud to your children?
- Do you feel a sense of fulfillment when you write poetry or volunteer in your community?

Once you figure out what makes you feel good about yourself, make those things a priority by implementing them into your every day or weekly schedule. No matter what makes sure you go out and do them! This may mean you have to give up other things to make time for them, but it also means that you may need to re-evaluate your schedule and life more so that you are doing what you honestly enjoy.

To ensure that you are doing these things, there are more than likely going to have to be actions you take to get to those happiness goals, such as saving money to buy supplies to paint, waking up an hour earlier, exercising more, etc.

It is important to realize that you need to do what you need to in order to fulfill your happiness goals. You cannot allow yourself to blame others if you do not fulfill these things. It is time to be a little selfish and fill up your own teapot so that you can fill up the cups of others in your life! This will help you to not only feel better and do better by other people, but it will help you to clear the fog on inconsistent negativity from your life and enable you to truly love yourself and your life once more

PART 2

Do you constantly find yourself doubting your own capabilities, being hard on yourself, always thinking you are not good enough? In this book, you will be introduced to self-compassion, what it is and what it isn't, the myths surrounding self-compassion and why it is worth introducing self-compassion in your life.

Reading and journeying through all the different chapters in this book, you will come to realize that it is about encouraging you to give self-compassion a try especially if you find yourself having negative thoughts and not giving yourself a break. It is easy to think that we are not good enough or we are not doing our best simply because we live in a culture of endless competition and striving and at times like this, self-compassion may seem like a luxury that none of us can afford but in truth, we can.

As a matter of fact, it is a luxury we cannot afford to live without. We need it because it helps us become better human beings to ourselves personally and to the people around us. In this book, you will see the different research that has been conducted showing how self-compassion ultimately leads us to life healthy lives, cultivate good habits, lower our depression and anxiety as well as have more satisfying relationships.

By cultivating self-compassion, you will be in a better position of assessing and acknowledging the challenges you are experiencing and develop more wise, thoughtful and helpful ways to respond. Self-compassion promotes understanding and acceptance on a personal and interpersonal level, in a way that encourages and empowers you to make positive change. By the end of this book, hopefully you have gathered enough information to help you be more self-compassionate and practice the necessary exercises to help promote self-compassionate in every aspect of your life.

Chapter 1- What is Self Compassion

What is the self-compassion? Have you thought about it or experienced it from someone?

The truth is, having compassion for yourself is not different from having compassion for other people or animals. Having self-compassion is being kind to yourself and understanding to your needs when you face personal failures. Think about how you would talk and console a friend who's going through a rough time- what would you say to them? Would you be harsh to them? Would you say things that bring them down even more?

The answers to those questions are of course a big NO. You would do what all good friends do- bring them up when they feel down, hug them and tell them everything is going to be ok, telling them that you'll be there for them to talk to or if they need help. Self-compassion is acting this same way towards yourself when you go through a rough patch. You notice the suffering and you empathize with yourself by comforting yourself, offering kindness and understanding.

Kristin D. Neff and Katie A. Dahm are two prominent are two names synonymous with the research on self-compassion. In their book, the Handbook of Mindfulness and Self-Regulation, it states that there are three primary components to self-compassion:

1. Self-kindness
2. Common humanity
3. Mindfulness

To understand self compassion, we need to consider what it means to feel compassion on a general level. Here are some views of compassion:

The Buddhist point of view of compassion is given to our own as well as to others suffering.

Goetz, Keltner & Simon- Thomans, 2010: Compassion is the sensitivity to the suffering that is happening, coupled with a deep desire to alleviate that suffering

Neff, 2003a: Self-compassion is compassion directed inwards, referring to ourselves as the object of concern and care when we are faced with an experience of suffering

The Three Elements of Self-Compassion

The key to understanding self-compassion is to understand the difference between this trait and more negative ones. Sometimes when we give ourselves self-compassion, it may be construed as narcissism to a point, which is why it is important to know what is self-compassion and to what degree is it considered self-compassion and when it isn't.

1. Self-kindness is not Self-Judgement

Self-compassion is being understanding and warm to ourselves when we fail, or when we suffer or at moments when we feel inadequate. We should not be ignoring these emotions or criticizing yourself. People who have self-compassion understand that being human comes with its own imperfections and failing is part of the human experience. It is inevitable that there will be no failure when we attempt something because failure is part of learning and progress. We will look into how failure is a friend in disguise in the next chapters. Having self-compassion is also being gentle with yourself when faced with painful experiences rather than getting angry at everything and anything that falls short of your goals and ideals.

Things cannot be exactly the way it should be or supposed to be or how we dream it to be. There will be changes and when we accept this with kindness and sympathy and understanding, we experience greater emotional equanimity.

2. Common humanity and not Isolation

It is a common human emotion to feel frustrated especially when things do not go the way we envision them to be. When this happens, frustration is usually accompanied by irrational isolation, making us feel and think that we are the only person on earth going through this or making dumb mistakes like this. News flash- all humans suffer, all of us go through different kinds of suffering at varying degrees. Self-compassion involves recognizing that we all suffer and all of us have personal inadequacies. It does not happen to 'Me' or 'I' alone.

3. Mindfulness is not Over-Identification

Self-compassion needs us to be balanced with our approach so that our negative emotions are neither exaggerated or suppressed. This balance act comes out from the process of relating our personal experiences with that of the suffering of others. This puts the situation we are going through into a larger perspective.

We need to keep mindful awareness so that we can observe our own negative thoughts and emotions with clarity and openness. Having a mindful approach is non-judgemental and it is a state of mindful reception that enables us to observe our feelings and thoughts without denying them or suppressing them. There is no way that we can ignore our pain and feel compassion at the same time. By having mindfulness, we also prevent over-identification of our thoughts and feelings.

Discovering Self Compassion

You're so dumb! You don't belong here loser! Those jeans make you look like a fat cow! You can't sit with us! It's safe to say we've all heard some kind rude, unwanted comments either directly or indirectly aimed at us. Would you talk like this to a friend? Again, the answer is a big NO.

Believe it or not, it is a lot easier and natural for us to be kind and nice to people than to be mean and rude to them whether it is a stranger or someone we care about in our lives. When someone we care is hurt or is going through a rough time, we console them and say it is ok to fail. We support them when they feel bad about themselves and we comfort them to make them feel better or just to give a shoulder to cry on.

We are all good at being understanding and compassionate and kind to others. How often do we offer this same kindness and compassion to ourselves? Research on self-compassion shows that those who are compassionate are less likely to be anxious, depressed or stressed and more resilient, happy and optimistic. In other words, they have better mental health.

Chapter 2: Benefits of Self-Compassion

You've probably heard your parents say time and time again to treat others as you would want them to treat you. Therefore, we are often taught to be empathetic and compassionate to others who are facing difficulties and challenges in their life. However, when faced with our own personnel challenges be it in our everyday lives, work and relationships, we often find ourselves becoming our own worst enemy. Hence we become too critical and judgmental on our own selves and in turn prevent any healing process from taking place.

Therefore, instead of being self-critical to oneself, we need to develop the concept of self-compassion in combating our negative thoughts and self-criticism that keeps us from overcoming our obstacles and challenges.

Self-compassion is defined as being compassionate to our own suffering, inadequacies, weakness and failures. As we know from the previous chapter, Kristin Neff, an associate professor at department of educational psychology in the University of Texas further breaks down self-compassion to 3 key elements which are self-kindness, common humanity and mindfulness.

Self-kindness is about recognizing our flaws and issues as well as being caring to oneself when going through bouts of hardship and challenges. Common humanity on the other hand, puts emphasis that the suffering and anguish we go through is all a natural part of being human and it's a normal part of everyday life. Lastly, mindfulness deals with the individual's ability to take a middle path in addressing their sufferings so as not to neglect or overthinking the situation.

Various research done on the topic of self-compassion indicates that individuals who practice self-compassion have a far greater psychological health than those who lack it. The individuals who practice self-compassion have a more positive life satisfaction, happiness and optimism. Apart from that self-compassion is also connected low levels of anxiety, self-criticism and depression. As such, in a way self-compassion can be used as a tool to develop inner strength when facing challenges in every aspect of our life.

So we know what self-compassion is and sure it helps us lead a better life and have better relationships. What other aspects of self-compassion are there? Here are some major benefits you can reap from being self-compassion. We explore it in terms of work, relationships and in life.

Self-Compassion At Work

Our daily work environment can be a long-lasting love-hate relationship with its own ups and downs that one has to face on a daily basis. As such, we are constantly bombarded with undue stress in meeting deadlines, reports and customer expectations. Many at times, we will face moments that completely overwhelm us and have a negative impact on us. This can be caused by numerous factors such as a negative remark by a colleague, superior or even a customer, failure to reach sales targets or goals, not getting that raise or promotion that you so deserve or even by making an unintentional mistake at the job. Since we all strive to achieve more and be perfect at our jobs, this negative circumstances will have an adverse effect if not dealt properly and swiftly.

Self-compassion can be used at work through the following means to reap various benefits: -

- Conducting a post-mortem to review the shortcomings and failures of a certain project or task and learning from these failures to prevent similar occurrences in the future.

- When facing criticism and rejection from colleagues, superiors and customers, instead of being self-critical and falling into complete despair, we will be able to be calm and focus our energies and thoughts of improving ourselves and not to allow stress to overwhelm ourselves.

- Applying self-compassion at work also helps us in being resilient through difficult scenarios especially is situations that we don't get a certain reward or promotion that we think we deserve.

- Self-compassion enables us to be more creative. When we fail a project or we do not complete a task or when a work event doesn't go as expected, being self-compassionate to ourselves will help us to look back at the series of events and instead of berating ourselves, we look back and see what we could have done better and learn from our mistakes. It makes us becoming more creative the next time around.

- Self-compassion builds trust. It enables you to be transparent and authentic, makes it easier for people to connect with you because you are your true self.

- Showing genuine compassion to yourself also means showing compassion to the people around you. When you show compassion to yourself, you extend this feeling to your co-workers and it makes them feel safe.

- Self compassion allows you to allow yourself and your team implicit permission to do their very best without worry of punishment or repercussions if something doesn't go right.

Self-Compassion In Relationships

In the topic of relationships be it a romantic or non-romantic relationship, we often find ourselves in situations of disagreement from time to time. And these can sometimes lead to moments of stress and unhappiness between oneself and their significant other/parent/sibling/friend. Self-compassion provides various ways much like our situations at work to help us deal with this issues and challenges. Many studies done on this matter point that self-compassion when used have the following positive impact on relationships: -

- Individuals who practice self-compassion know that every individual as well as themselves aren't perfect and are subjected to weaknesses and shortcomings

- They are able relate to their partners much better

- They are more warm and compassionate in understanding a situation

- They are more open to compromising to resolve a situation
- Individuals who are self-compassionate have better empathy. The bring out the best in their partners.
- They are more responsive and aware to the issues that their partner faces
- They are better listeners, they listen to understand and not answer
- People who practice self-compassion own up to their mistakes

Studies also have shown that individuals that lack self-compassion tend to have a negative effect on people around them which may lead to isolation. As such, those people who practice self-compassion have healthier and happier relationships and have a bigger a wide social circle.

Self-Compassion In Life

When encountering difficulties in daily life which can range from a number of issues/aspects such as health to financial issues, we need to act by being compassionate and kind to ourselves. When faced with various issues on a daily basis, self-compassion allows us to look for solutions to take care of oneself instead of berating or being overly critical of one's lack of accomplishments or weaknesses.

With that being said, an individual who practices self-compassion will look into various ways to engage their mind and body into healthy activities that can stimulate them and lets them focus on positive aspects instead of groveling on a negative situation. This can be in a form of an exercise, a hobby, prayer or even a warm bath or a cup of tea to calm themselves down.

Self-compassionate individuals tend to be more: -

- Happier
- Satisfied with life
- Resilient
- Emotionally intelligent
- Have better coping mechanisms
- Optimistic
- Creative
- Less judgemental
- Better goal-getters
- It greatly reduces mental problems

As such, cultivating the habits of self-compassion in every aspect of our life will allow to become the best version of ourselves and allow us to live much happier with the right mindset.

SELF LOVE

Chapter 3- Myths about Self Compassion

Many people do not have any issues with showing compassion to other people- it is a commendable quality. Compassion is often seen with kindness, tenderness, understanding, sympathy, empathy and of course the impulse to help those in need, whether human or animal.

However, with self-compassion, that is a different story altogether. For plenty of people, having self-compassion often relates to negative qualities such as self-serving, self-pity, self-centered, indulgent and just selfish. We seem to think that if we are not hard on ourselves or punishing ourselves over our failures and flaws, we risk a runaway ego and fall into the traps of false pride.

Take for example, Norman. A young bank executive who is also a new father. Between juggling work and a new baby, he also spends time volunteering as a football coach at a local shelter. He is a committed father and husband, a hard worker and a community role-model. But Norman has gone through several episodes of anxiety attacks simply because he feels overwhelmed, he feels he isn't contributing enough in his team at work and isn't good enough as a husband or father.

People have misgivings about self-compassion and it is only because nobody really knows what it looks like, or even how to practice it so it doesn't become excessive and borderline narcissistic. Self compassion has the element of mindfulness, of wisdom and the recognition to common humanity. Research by Kristin Neff points the myths that people have on self-compassion is the main reason why most of us are in the cycle of criticizing yourself over and over again. Here are the common myths:

#1 Self-Compassion is just a person crying out for self-pity

Let's get this straight- self compassion does not mean you are feeling sorry for yourself. It is fact an antidote to self-pity. It isn't about whining about our bad luck but instead, self-compassion makes us more open to acknowledging. accepting and experiencing difficult feelings with the help of kindness. Self-compassionate people have a lower tendency of wallowing in self-pity about how bad the circumstances may be and this leads to better mental clarity and mental health.

Filip Raes of the University of Leuven conducted a study on the connection between self-compassion, mental health and ruminative thinking. This study was conducted among the students in his university. Students were first assessed using the Self-Compassion Scale developed by Dr. Kristin Neff. Participants were asked how often they responded to behaviors that corresponded with the main components of self-compassion. These behaviors included "I try to be patient and understanding towards the elements of my personality that I am not fond of"; "When things are going badly for me, I see them as part of life that happens to everyone".

The result of the study showed that students who had better self-compassion parameters were less whiny and broody when things did not go their way. They were also less anxious and less depressed and showed better signs of attentiveness.

#2 Self-compassion is a sign of weakness

Melissa, as a first born child was always seen as the responsible one, a label she has taken on with pride. She sees herself as a pillar of strength to her family. However, since Melissa got married, she has decided to take a step back and pay more attention to her new marriage. While her own family has never imposed on her, Melissa secretly feels as if she is not being a good daughter, and racked with guilt. When her friends suggested that she try not being too hard on herself, her reaction was to immediately tell them off, saying that self-compassion does not make her a good daughter. What Melissa does not know is that this is not a sign of her abandoning her family or a sign of weakness but discovering self-compassion is part of the process of resilience to us. When going through changes in life, self-compassion enables us to survive and thrive.

#3 Self-Compassion can make you a complacent person

Thinking that self-compassion makes you complacent is one of the biggest blocks you can place on yourself. It's so easy for us to criticize ourselves just because we fail to live up to certain standards and we immediately label ourselves as sloths. Do we do this to our kids too?

Amanda's daughter just failed her Biology test and upon finding out, Amanda starts berating her, saying that she is stupid and that she is ashamed of her. This is the exact same thing that Amanda tells herself when she fails to live up to a certain expectation. Rather than motivating her daughter, these comments on her daughter lose faith in herself and prevents her from trying to do better.

What Amanda can do however is practice a more compassionate approach to the situation by giving a hug, telling her daughter that it happens to anyone and what support can she give her daughter. Telling her daughter that she believes in her will help motivate her.

Amanda needs to give honest recognition to the failure as well as empathize with her daughter's unhappiness. This caring response helps us boost out self-confidence and spread emotional support.

While Amanda may not have said those words to her daughter, she still believes deep down that this type of negative feedback may spur her daughter to achieve the necessary goals. But thanks research on human emotions and its responses, showing self-compassion is more effective to boost a better rate of success than self-punishment.

Juliana Breines and Serena Chen of University of California conducted a research to examine the effects of self-compassion and to see how or if it was one of the factors that motivated participants to get involved in positive behaviors and make positive changes. Participants were ask to think back at a time when they felt guilty about such as lying to a partner, cheating in an exam which made them feel bad even till now. They were then randomly assigned to write to themselves from three different perspectives:

1. that of a compassionate and understanding friend
2. write about their own positive qualities
3. write about a hobby they enjoyed doing

Researchers found that participants involved in the self-compassionate perspective were more remorseful for their wrong doing and were more motivated to not repeat the offence.

The research concluded that self-compassion was not about evading personal accountability, rather strengthening it. Acknowledging our failures with kindness rather than judgements enables us to see ourselves clearly beyond the spectacles of self-judgement. Tell ourselves 'I can't believe I messed up. I got so stressed and I overreacted' rather than 'I cannot believe i said that. Why am I so mean?'

#4 Self-Compassions makes us more narcissistic

To many Americans, having high self-esteem means that you are special and beyond average. For some people with high self-esteem, the minute that we receive a less than average score, our self-esteem crashes and plummets. There is no way that everyone to be above average all the time. There are some areas that we can excel because we are naturally good at it but then there are aspects that we either under perform or we are just average. That is why diversity is good. At times when we do perform below average, we see ourselves like failures. The desire to be above average is always going to be there, as we like that feeling of high self-esteem. However this can make us be develop nasty behaviors.

Jean Twenge, a researcher from the San Diego University and Keith Campbell from the University of Georgia have been studying narcissism scores since 1987 among college students. It may not come as a surprise to you to know that among modern-day social media savvy students, narcissism ran high.

It is extremely important to note the difference between self-compassion and self-esteem. While they are both connected to our psychological well-being, the difference is very vivid:

- Self-esteem is evaluating your self-worth positively
- Self-compassion is relating to the changes that happen to us with kindness and acceptance

With self-esteem, we want to feel better than the people around us but with self-compassion, we acknowledge the fact that we have and share certain imperfections. Self-esteem is buoyancy, depending on our latest success or failure. Those with higher levels of self-esteem tend to get upset when they receive neutral feedback. They often start thinking 'Am I just average? I thought i was exceptional'. They are also likelier to listen to any feedback that is related to their personality and blame it on external factors. Self-esteem thrives only when the reviews are good which leads to evasiveness.

Self-compassionate people on the other hand are more emotionally stable despite the degree of praise they receive.

#5 Self-compassion makes us selfish

It is easy to conflate self-compassion with selfishness. Joshua for example spends a large portion of his day caring for his family and at weekends, he supports activities at the local college. He was raised in a family placed importance on service to others. This eventually led him to think that spending time for self-care and being kind and caring to his needs meant he must be neglecting the people around him just for his own needs.

There are plenty of people like Joshua- selfless, good, altruistic and generous to others but horrible to their own selves. When we become too absorbed in self-judgement, we end up giving less because we are preoccupied by thinking about our inadequacies and worthless selves.

Plenty of our emotional needs are met when we are kind and nurturing to ourselves which leaves us in a better position to focus on the people around us. However, caring for the welfare of others often becomes a bigger priority and the idea of treating ourselves badly starts rearing its ugly head. Think about the safety message on an airplane. It is advised to place the oxygen mask over your ownself before assisting others right? This is the same for self compassion.

Kristin Neff conducted a research with Tasha Beretvas of the University of Texas just to prove that being good to ourselves is more helpful when we want to be good to others. The research look at whether people who were self-compassionate were more giving in their relationships.It explored 100 couple who are in romantic relationships for a year or longer. Participants were asked to rate themselves based on the Self-Compassion Scale.

Neff & Beretvas found that partners who were self-compassionate individuals were described as more accepting, caring and supportive compared to self-critical partners who were seen as detached, controlling and aggressive. Self-compassionate partners brought to the table a more secure and satisfied relationship.

A growing research also focuses on therapists and caregivers who were more self-compassionate. Those who were were less likely to feel caregiver burnout and they were more satisfied with their careers, they were more happy, they felt more energized and were more grateful to be able to make a difference.

Conclusion

Self-compassion enables us to feel love, courage, wisdom and generosity in a more sustainable way. It gives us a boundless and directionless mental and emotional state. The power of self-compassion can be enriched through practice and of course through learning, just like so many other good habits.

Being kind to ourselves is not a selfish luxury or a sign of weakness or self-pity. It is a gift to our persons to make us happier and more fulfilled. Thanks to the many research conducted, we now know the myths of self-compassion.

Chapter 4- Dealing with Negativity

Did you ever realize that it is much easier to be happy than it is to be unhappy? Go ahead. Think about it. While you are reading this, just think about the many things that happened before you opening this book and reading. What happened when you woke up? Did you get a kiss from your partner? How did your coffee taste this morning? How is the weather outside like now? All these things that happened to you today, what made you happy and what made you sad?

If you listed ten things today and 7 of them were things that made your happy and three made you unhappy, sad, frustrated or moody, then most likely you were grateful, and you were positive. The thing is, many of us would prefer to be happy and positive rather than be unhappy and negative. And it is that simple to be positive and happy. Also, positive thinking is above and beyond just being happy or displaying a cheerful and upbeat attitude. It also creates and establishes value in your life and relationships, and it also helps you build skills that benefit you longer than your smile can take you. Barbara Fredrickson, a positive psychology researcher from the University of North Carolina, published a landmark paper on the impact of positive thinking on work, health and general wellbeing. Here's a little brief of Barbara's research:

What Can Negative Thinking do to your Brain?

Our brain is programmed to respond to negative emotions by shutting off the world around us and limiting the options we see around us. For example, if you get into a fight with your sister, your emotions and anger might consume to the point where you react adversely- you can't think about anything else. Or for instance your coffee this morning spilled on your shirt, and this creates a domino effect of everything going wrong in your day, and you get so stressed out that you find it hard to start or do anything because you've lost your focus. Or if you are supposed to complete a project but you didn't, you start to feel bad about it and all you think is how irresponsible you are and that you are lazy, and you lack motivation. The point is, our brain shuts off from the outside world and relies on the negative emotions of fear, stress, and anger. Negative thoughts and emotions prevent us from seeing other options, solutions or choices that are around us.

What Can Positive Thinking do to your Brain?

Barbara Fredrickson also explains how positive thinking manifests in our brain. She explains with an experiment where research subjects are divided into five groups, and each group is shown a different video clip. The first group was shown clips that created feelings of joy whereas the second group was shown clips that created contentment, the third was the control group that had images of no significant emotions and were neutral whereas group four had clips that created fear and group five had clips that created the feelings of anger.

Participants were then asked to imagine themselves in situations that these same emotions would come about and write down their reactions to it. Participants that viewed images of fear and anger had the least responses or reactions whereas participants who saw joy and contentment had more reactions. The bottom line is, if you experience positive emotions you will see more possibilities in life. Positive emotions broaden our possibilities and thinking, thus opening up more options for us in facing issues, crisis, problems, and solutions and so on. In the next few chapters, we will discuss how we can work our mind to be more positive and look at things in a more positive perspective to enhance and give more value to our life, relationships, and goals. It is not as hard as it seems because all it takes is a little practice.

Have you seen the movie Inside Out?

If you did, then you will probably realize that being sad is a good thing-not always, but this emotion is there for a reason. When we talk about dealing with negativity, it doesn't necessarily mean being optimistic all the time, especially in the face of suffering.

Pain and sadness are just part of the complex human emotions all of us have, and it is just as important to feel pain and sadness, guilt and fear as this are all part and parcel of coping. Experiencing and processing negative emotions in a healthy way is a crucial part of personal growth.

There are two scenarios when people are confronted with negative situations. One, they either obsess over the problem or two, they numb their emotions. Either of these coping methods is not healthy, and it can create harmful patterns in our mind, over a period of time. Obsessing is deceptive because it feels as if you are thinking things through but to continuously obsess over a situation only reinforces the impact of the negative thoughts and emotions.

That said, numbing your emotions towards a pained situation isn't good either because it really is not possible to selectively numb out an emotion. Humans are so complex that our range of emotions does not enable us to directly shut down an emotion. If you somehow blot out anger, you'll blur out happiness and serenity too. Why? Because while you like being active and optimistic all the time, not showing anger to something that has hurt you or pained you or frustrated you, will make you feel more bitter eventually. Only because you weren't able to express your anger, the situation or the person related to this will not know how you feel. For example, if we use alcohol to numb our pain, we do not learn how to cope with sadness. We just develop another problem which is alcohol abuse.

If you are going through a pained time, then you need to develop healthy coping skills, and this involves recognizing the inevitability and necessity of some suffering and moving on from it. The process usually includes:

- Acknowledging your negative feelings and watch them with a non-judgmental attitude
- Recognize when they are triggered and assess your reactions when responding to this
- Understand that pain is just a catalyst for growth and resilience
- Practice forgiveness towards those who have pained you
- Express yourself in creative and healthy ways like painting or exercising
- Seek the support of others

Steps to deal with Negative thoughts and Events

Here are some tried and tested ways to overcome negative thoughts and events which you can try:

1. Meditate or do yoga.

Yoga helps take your focus away from your thoughts and bring attention to your breath. Yoga or meditation is very relaxing, and it helps ease one's mind. It also helps you stay present and focused on the moment that is happening.

2. Smile.

Pain and sadness can make it very hard to smile. While it does seem hard to smile when you aren't feeling so happy inside, you need to sometimes force this out of you. So try doing this in front of a mirror everyday or make a mental note to smile to the people you correspond with daily.

3. Surround yourself with positive people.

Surround yourself with friends and family that can give you constructive and loving feedback. Each time you feel you are going down into your negative spiral, call these people up and speak to them so they can put your focus back again to where it's needed to be at the time.

4. Change your thoughts from negative to positive.

Easier said than done, no doubt but you can turn any situation into a positive one. For example, if you have just started a new job you barely have enough experience of, instead of saying 'I'll take a long time to adjust or learn' just say 'I will take on any challenges because challenges excite me!'

5.   Don't wallow in self-pity. Take charge of your life

You are the captain of your shop so do not make yourself a victim. There is always a way out of any situation so if it becomes to unbearable, then leave. Otherwise, you stay put and make the best of it and don't point fingers, blame, complain or whine.

6.   Volunteer

Volunteering also takes the focus away. If you think you are in a bad situation, imagine the people who need food aid or money. Do something nice for someone else so volunteer at an organization or donate.

7.   Remember to keep moving forward

We easily dwell on our mistakes and feel terrible for the way we acted. But you can't reverse the situation so instead of feeling sorry for yourself or beating yourself up over what you'd done, tell yourself that you'd made a mistake, you learned from it, and you want to move on.

8.   Listen to music

One of the best ways to alleviate your mood especially in the morning is by listening to songs and singing in the shower! It doesn't matter if you remember the lyrics – a good happy song will put you in a good and happy mood.

9.   Be grateful

Being grateful enables you to appreciate all the things you have. So be grateful every day.

10. Read positive quotes.

Just log into Pinterest, read positive quotes every day. Better yet, print out the ones that you like and stick in on your wall, your fridge or your computer.

Learn to Forgive Yourself

Just like negative emotions, failure is also good to experience because it only makes us stronger.

Yes! Failure is something that didn't kill you. You're still alive! So what doesn't kill you only makes you stronger. Why do you need experience failure? Nobody wants to experience failure but if you looked at the successful people in our generation today, or even the past- they all failed. They all made mistakes. They all went through trial and error. What sets them apart from the perennial failures? They didn't give up. They learnt from their mistakes. They had extreme passion, making them eager to keep on trying till they succeeded. Here's why you need to experience failure:

- Without failure, you'd be sucked into a blissful feeling that nothing can go wrong and that everything you'd put into place will work exactly as how it should be
- When something does go wrong, you are unable to cope with the change or adapt to create solutions.
- Failure enables us to work on our flaws and it also allows us to right our wrongs. Failure also enables us upgrade or enhance or refine our work, technique and solutions

- Failure also teaches us a lesson. It is our choice to learn from it or run from it

When we fail, it's easy to get discouraged and upset and we develop a sense of being afraid to fail again. In order to be successful in anything that we do, we just need to remind ourselves to let go of our pride and ego. Failure only makes us grow wiser, make us more adaptable and vivid to any possible scenarios that could happen. We are more prepared to face the same problem but at a different angle.

So how do you look at failure at a positive way? We need to redefine the way we view failure. The fear of failure is what stops many great individuals from creating something beneficial and meaningful in our world. The fear of failure is why we stop ourselves from living extraordinary lives.

The fear of failure is why we never submitted the novel we wrote, we never expressed our feelings to the people we love, never bungee jumped or telling someone how you really feel.

Daniel Epstein, founder of Unreasonable group stresses the point of re-branding the way we see failure. He suggests defining it as such:

"To Fail means "to not start doing something you believe in. To stop doing something you believe in just because it is hard. To ignore your gut instinct around what you believe is right and wrong."

In actual fact, many of the world's greatest philosophers, entrepreneurs, scientists and artisans have all expressed their thoughts on failure and how it has helped them overcome adversity and obstacles. All these perceptions tell us that fear of failure is evident in every human being but with passion and perseverance to achieve what you want will be the driving force in the determination between constant failure and success.

Hopefully, these quotes will give you a good perspective. After all, what better way to learn than to be inspired by some of the most successful people on earth?

Remembering that I'll be dead soon is the most important tool I've ever encountered to help me make the big choices in life. Because almost everything – all external expectations, all pride, all fear of embarrassment or failure – these things just fall away in the face of death, leaving only what is truly important. ~Steve Jobs

I've missed more than 9000 shots in my career. I've lost almost 300 games. 26 times, I've been trusted to take the game winning shot and missed. I've failed over and over and over again in my life. And that is why I succeed. ~Michael Jordan

Our doubts are traitors, and make us lose the good we oft might win, by fearing to attempt. ~William Shakespeare

For every failure, there's an alternative course of action. You just have to find it. When you come to a roadblock, take a detour. ~Mary Kay Ash

Failure is blindness to the strategic element in events; success is readiness for instant action when the opportune moment arrives. ~Newell D. Hillis

The only real failure in life is not to be true to the best one knows. ~Buddha

Success is often achieved by those who don't know that failure is inevitable. ~Coco Chanel

Steps to Overcome Failure

Highly successful people are the ones who have failed the most. We only hear about their successes but never the trials and tribulations and obstacles that they had to go through. Setbacks and failures are part of life and nobody is perfect. Yes we fall into hard times at some point in our lives but what this is all a lesson to us. If we can manage it effectively, then no matter what comes our way in the future, we can overcome it. Here are four steps that can help you turn any negative experience into a positive one:

- **Failure is part of the road to success-** When times get tough, the tough get going. It is frustrating to hear people tell us to be positive when we are faced with adversity but this doesn't mean we have to be smiling all the time or be happy all the time. Staying positive is knowing that despite your setback, you can bounce back again. Staying positive is learning and growing and evolving. Understand that setbacks aren't the end of the road; rather it is carving a step in our journey to succeed. When life hits you with a setback, its okay to be sad and frustrated and upset- but we should never stay down.

- **Blow your Steam off-** When you hit a setback or a failure, your mind gets clouded. You worked so hard to get to this point, only to fail. If you have come to this point, take a step back and evaluate your work. Take some time off to clear your head and accept your mistakes. Once you have done this, you will begin to accept what has happened and how it happened or why it happened. This emotional state will eventually evaporate and then you can go back to focus on the work at hand.

- **Be Honest-** Being brutally honest to ourselves in the midst of a failure is a trait of success. Most people do not want to admit their mistake or admit that it is their own fault that all these negative scenarios have happened. The thing is, part of being positive is also about being responsible and being accountable to ourselves and the mistakes we have made. We need to do this because this is how we learn. Albert Einstein once said that it is crazy to keep doing the same thing over and over again and expecting different results. That is why learning from our mistakes is a crucial part of moving on and part of learning. If we do not learn from our mistakes, we are doomed to be repeating them again and again and again.

- **Move Forward-** We need to move forward each time we fail. When we fail, we fail forward which means learning from our setbacks and then, making the necessary adjustments until we reach success. You have come so far, do not give up. So each change we make, each person we meet and every tiny bit of information we learn all combines to create a different outcome for us to learn from.

Obstacles are inevitable in life but there are always two ways of handling them. While they may block your focus out temporarily, our perseverance is the element that determines whether we fall back or move forward. As we get more and more efficient in the journey of positive thinking, we will enable ourselves to always see the positive side of things even in the most darkest of situations or the hardest of times.

Surrounding yourself with Positive People

No doubt that people have a huge impact on your life. According to Jim Rohn, American entrepreneur and motivation speaker, we all spend our time with an average of five people. With this in mind, think about who these 5 people are and how they impact your life.

Some people, including your friends whom you've known for a long time, can be parasites. These parasites suck out your energy and happiness and even your resources.

So what makes someone a 'good' person you can spend your time with? What are the benefits of surrounding yourself with self-disciplined people?

Your GOOD Category

The people around you can be good in so many ways. This doesn't mean that they go to church every Sunday. It's more like feeding the poor, looking after abandon dogs or something simple like encouraging you to hit the gym more often. These people can be your friends, your family, your co-workers and even some acquaintances.

In essence, good people are productive people. They have a lot of good traits in them that inspire and motivate you too.

It is also important to note too much of something good can also inhibit your growth. You need diversity and healthy arguments and discussions along the way. Always be eager to learn new knowledge and look at different perspectives from your peers.

Think About How You Interact with People

Time for a little exercise. Write down the names of the five people you usually spend time with. Then, write down the qualities you see in them. Think about how they positively or negatively affect you. Are you happy around them? Do they make you feel like you got what it takes to reach your goals? Do they support you? If your list has more positives than negatives, then you probably have the good people around you.

You want to surround yourself with people who make you happy, with those that make you feel alive, the people who help you when you are in need and those that make you feel safe- they are the ones who genuinely care and are worth keeping in your life.

The key here is to finding what is good for you because what is good for you may be different for someone else.

So how do you do that?

Your vibe is what will attract the people around you. When you give off good vibes, good vibes will follow you. You will also feel less stressed and find joy even in the most simplest things like the blue sky or a scoop of vanilla ice cream.

So train your mind to not think negatively and try to see the positive side of things. It is ok to feel sadness and grief and bitterness when things don't go the way you want or something bad happens but if you start building a home in the negativity scene, it'll be harder for you to leave it.

Today, make a commitment to start spending more time with the good people in your life.

Benefits of surrounding yourself with Positive People

1.   You Do not get into needless battles

Thoughts become things- you've heard it before. But some of these things are also feelings and feelings are energy. The feelings of happiness, sadness, gratitude, confidence are all energy- negative and positive. When you surround yourself with positive people, you eliminate negative energy, thus eliminate unnecessary conflicts.

2.   You get to live in the feeling of gratitude more frequently

People who are happy will genuinely be happy for you when you make it big or achieve your goal. Surrounding yourself with unsuccessful people and then talking about your successes will only remind these people of what they don't have. By contrast, surrounding yourself with people that have more than what you have you will make you feel more gratitude frequently. Gratitude is the attitude that brings success.

For example, if you achieved your goal in achieving a healthy, physically toned body, you're not going to be telling this to someone who is overweight (by choice) right? Because that person will only think you are bragging and wont share in your good fortune.

3.   You get to be someone you've never been

In order to do something you have never done before, you need to stop caring about what people think of you. You need to realize that you cannot be doing the same things you have done if you want to become someone better. Surrounding yourself with people who want to achieve the same goal as you can make you do things you otherwise will not do. Successful people recognize that change is inevitable and that it must take place. Unsuccessful people will begrudge the changes in you whereas successful people will be glad that it happened and welcome it.

Chapter 5- Building and Mastering Emotions

Being aware of our emotions also means knowing that our emotions can drive our behavior and impact those around us, either positively or negatively. It also means we have the ability to manage these emotions, that of our own and that of others, especially at pressuring and stressful times.

The Five Categories of Emotional Intelligence (EQ)

When it comes to Emotional Intelligence, there are five categories that becomes a focus.

1. Self-awareness.

Having self-awareness means having the ability to recognize an emotion as and when it occurs and it is the key to your EQ. In order to develop self-awareness, a person needs to tune into their own true feelings, evaluating them and subsequently managing them.

In self-awareness, the important elements are:

- Recognizing our own own emotions and its effects
- Having a level of confidence and sureness of your capabilities and your self-worth

2. Self-regulation.

When we experience emotions, we often have little control over our actions when we first feel these emotions. One thing we can control however is how long these emotions last. To control how long certain emotions last, especially negative ones, certain methods are used to lessen the effects of these emotions such as anxiety, anger and even depression. These methods include reinventing a scenario in a much positive manner such as through taking a long walk, saying a prayer and even meditating.

Self-regulation includes:

- Innovation which means open to new ideas
- Adaptability to handle change and be flexible
- Trustworthiness referring to the ability to keep to standards of integrity and honesty
- Taking responsibility, conscientiousness of our own actions
- Self-control to prevent disruptive impulses

3. Motivation

Having motivation is what keeps us going to accomplish our tasks and goals and to maintain an air of positivity. With practice and with effort, we can all program our minds to be more positive although as human beings, it is also good to be negative at times. This does not mean having negative thoughts are bad, but these thoughts need to be kept in check as they cause more harm than good. Whenever you feel like you have negative feelings, you can also reprogram them to be more positive or at least to pick out the positive aspects of the situation, the silver lining which will help you be more focused in solving the problem.

Motivation is made up of:

- Having the sense of achievement drive, to constantly strive to improve and meet a level of excellence.
- Having the commitment to align your individual, group or organizational goals
- Having the initiative to act on available opportunities
- Having the optimism to pursue your goals persistently and objectively, despite the setbacks and obstacles.

4. Empathy

Empathy is the ability to recognize how people would feel towards a certain scenario, thing or person. Having this ability is crucial to success both in career as with life. The more you can decipher the feelings of people, the better you can manage the thoughts and approaches you send them. Empathetic people are excellent at:

- Recognizing, anticipating and meeting a person's needs
- Developing the needs of other people and bolstering their individual abilities
- Taking advantage of diversity by cultivating opportunities among different people
- Developing political awareness by understanding the current emotional state of people and fostering powerful relationships
- Focusing on identifying feelings and wants of other people

5. Social skills.

Developing good interpersonal skills is imperative as well if you want a successful life and a successful career. In our world today when plenty of thing are digitized, social skills seem to be an afterthought. People skills are more relevant and sought-after then before especially since now you also need a high EQ understand, negotiate and empathize with others especially if you deal and interact with different people on a daily basis. Among the most useful skills are:

- Influence to effectively wield persuasive tactics
- Communication to send our clear and concise messages
- Leadership to inspire and guide people and groups.
- Change catalyst in kick-starting and managing change
- Managing conflicting situations which includes the ability to negotiate, understand and resolve disagreements
- To bond and nurture meaningful and instrumental relationships
- Teamwork, cooperation and collaboration in meeting shared goals
- Creating a synergetic group to work towards collective goals.

Creating a Balance with Emotional Awareness

As a human being, emotions and feelings make up every aspect of our existence. Managing them and keeping them balanced will help us reach our maximum potential in life, at work and especially in our relationships. As we know by now, having good emotional balance leads us towards better physical and mental health, making life happier.

When our emotional well-being is disrupted, this will result in the opposite. Our physical health will decline, we will start having digestive problems, lack of energy and sleep issues. People with emotional distress often exhibit low self-esteem, they are self-critical and pessimistic. They always need to assert themselves through their behavior. They are overly worried, get afraid very fast and they are focused on the past.

● Connection between our Thoughts and Feelings

Thoughts determine our feelings and they are nothing more than firing the neurons in our body. Our thoughts also generate feelings, making our body release additive natural substances such as cortisol and adrenaline.

The connection between the body and the mind is extremely vivid and strong, strong enough that the mental and physical state sends positive and negative vibes both ways. The feelings we experience depends on our thought, combined with our attitudes and actions.

Emotions are part of our daily life and we experience this everyday. What we want is to strike a balance in our emotions, thoughts and feelings to ensure that they do not adversely affect our daily tasks and cause us stress.

● Creating Emotional Balance

So how we do create emotional balance? Emotional balance is the ability to maintain equilibrium and flexibility between the mind and body when we are faced with changes or challenges. Here are some ways that you can create emotional balance:

1. Accept your emotions

Many of our mental, emotional and physical problems stem from our inability to express ourselves emotionally. When we experience an emotional distraught, we smother it in the comforts of eating, sleeping, sweating it out, sucking it up, it is swept under a rug, we bury it, project it elsewhere, meditate even all in the hopes of suppressing our emotions instead of actually dealing with it by accepting that this is what we are going through right not. The key here is to allow ourselves unconditional permission to feel- to cry when we want to, to feel anger when we are angry, sadness when we grief and so on. Let your guard down either when you are alone or with someone you trust and just focus on the feeling and situation. Experience and immerse yourself in this feeling so you can comprehend better why it hurts and what you will be doing to remedy the situation once you've accepted and acknowledge these feelings.

2. Express yourself

Expressing yourself is important. There are many ways to express oneself and usually when we experience a feeling, we react by crying, shouting, throwing things. But to identify with ourselves and be able to manage our emotions properly, we can also express ourselves through more positive ways. Some people like reading as it provides an escape into a different world. Some people express themselves through art or music. Whatever it is that you do, make sure you stay connected to discover more about yourself, your identity and also the person you want to become.

3.   Don't shove your feelings

Sometimes, it is easy to shove our feelings and not think about it, especially painful and scary memories. But as we all know, stuffing your memories and feelings will only make things worse for you. While it is hard to address your fears and sadness, rage and anger, once you actually dive into it, you will find that it will become easier to face your fears and eventually, the choppy waters will become calmer.

Be accepting your past and dealing with it in a more emotional state, you ultimately will lead a harmonious life. Always allow yourself to feel because your reactions to these different feelings would be in a more stable way rather than an overreaction.

4.   See the world in a positive light

It is easier said than done, we know. In a world full of hatred, sadness, grief, war, crime, unfairness- it is a threat to our emotional health. You tend to develop low self-esteem and start asking yourself if you are worth it, if you can get through it, if you are doing things right and all these thinking steers you towards making more mistakes and missteps. Rather than having emotional self-doubt, take action to develop a prerogative of seeing the world in a more positive light.

Do not feel responsible for the bad things that happen which is not caused by you is a good start. Have compassion in yourself and practice mindfulness and accept that occasional lapses and failures are just part of being human.

5. Get a grip on your mind

The way we think causes us emotional distress- this probably is not news to you. We all have this tendency into overthinking and these thoughts that do not serve you or give you any positivity is just setting you up for emotional distress. So get a grip on your mind- do not let it wander to much especially when you start overthinking.

6. Practice Yoga and Mindfulness

Doing yoga on a daily basis does help in your mental health- it helps by increasing your confidence in your abilities and it also helps you make better, definitive decisions.

You also learn to not be so self-criticizing. Yoga, practiced on a daily basis can help get rid of negative energy within you and help you work your way towards mental clarity and vital energy.

Not only that, the breathing that is practiced in yoga helps you relax better, make you calmer especially if your mind is racing and it also helps you to refine your feelings.

Breathing correctly helps you get rid of stress and anxiety as well.

Conclusion

While emotional balance is vital, just remember that it is alright to have emotional imbalance so do not beat yourself up over it and overthink things. However, do not neglect this imbalance. If you feel you are emotionally imbalanced, do something about it either talk to someone you trust, meet a therapist or just find a positive way to express your emotions and feelings. Live a life without or little regrets.

Chapter 6- Practical steps for Becoming self compassionate

Self-compassion is necessary for a healthy relationship, healthy mind and healthy body. How we interact with people and how we think affects how our body responds too. Self-compassion is the practice of goodwill and not good feelings. To practice self-compassion, we have first and foremost, change the way we think and perceive things. We also need a little bit of faith and believe in ourselves, in our strengths, in the way our life is heading, our goals and our priorities.

In this chapter, we will look at:

- the power of faith and believe in changing our perceptions
- practising creative visualization
- Practising affirmations
- **Faith & Believe**

When someone says 'Have faith' this depends on what you view or think what faith is. For many people, faith can be many different things and in all honesty, there's no right or wrong.

Conventionally, a lot of people associate faith with spirituality or the faith in God and that's not wrong either but like mentioned above, the very fact that people have different perspectives of what faith is is a good thing! It is quite enlightening and helpful to plenty of individuals that faith has different meanings as it can help different people make clearer sense of the various spectrums of life.

Here's a quick guideline to what faith means:

- **Faith**

Faith can mean faith in a supreme being, in God. But psychologists of religion would say that this is more of belief. Faith, in a more naturalistic and psychological sense, is really about the innate sense to search for meaning, purpose, and significance. Every human person has a strong sense that there is more than what meets the eye. In other words, there is something more than just 'me' and as human beings, we all discover what this might be- some of us go all out while some of us are content with the information we have at the moment.

All of us human beings seek out to find the deeper meaning, purpose and significance that exist in our lives, in our relationships and all the things that occur around us. This is the very basic striving of faith and the universal role it plays in our lives.

Wikipedia describes faith as a trust or confidence on a person, element or thing. Faith also is connected to the observation of an obligatory process that creates loyalty or even fidelity to a person, a promise or engagement. Faith is also a belief that is not based on facts and proof and faith can also mean loyalty to a system of religious belief.

While we think that only people that belief in divine intervention or God seem to have faith, the thing is even atheists have this kind of faith- a belief or trust or confidence. Everyone has the gift of faith- some of us have strong faith while some of us have weaker faith, but it really depends on the context we talk about.

- **Belief**

This brings us to the next element- belief. Belief is a representation of truth claims that you make on your spiritual journey. Beliefs are what tell you what is true and what is not true, and this is based on your experiences to satisfy your sense of faith. Your beliefs are what your hold to be true in your journey to satisfy your faith by engaging in various spiritual pursuits such as pilgrimage.

- **The Value of Faith**

While we all like to think we have faith (and high levels of it) the truth is, the value of our faith only grows when we are faced with troubling times. Many people believe that their faith value is determined by the evidence of things or successful moments or achievements in life. But the value of faith only increases as we grow older, as we experience more and more things in life, some good and some bad. Our faith becomes more valuable as we go through the trials and testaments of life and its heartaches. It is only during these times that you truly understand the depth and strength of a person's faith.

- **The Difference between Faith & Belief**

Probably by reading this now, you'd come to deduce that faith and belief are not the same things. In fact, in most cases, faith and belief are entirely the opposite of each other. Confusion between these two elements is tested when you face a crisis. While you may be searching for faith in something at a moment of crisis, you may be only pulling out the various beliefs that you have.

So the question is, who are you if not for your convictions?

If you have gone through a terrible crisis in life, you are probably still trying to figure it all out. Some people take years to understand why what happened to them, happened. Many people, especially those who are religious, feel the need to leave their faith in God because they believe that God has abandoned them.

But the questions are, were you abandoned by God or were you abandoned by your beliefs?

- **Belief as a product of the Mind**

A negative mind is already at a disadvantage but even a healthy mind can run into its own set of problems. For the enabled mind, a person may think that because they pray to God, all their prayers will be answered and that God is just and he will set things right. The positive mind will say that if we hold on to our beliefs strongly, God listens and will favor us.

But what is it that we believe in? Our beliefs are rooted in our culture and our upbringing. This is the first thing that separates our faith from our belief. Oftentimes, what we belief in may directly contradict everything else we know to be true and right. It can be universally acknowledged that we arrive at the crossroads of faith and belief when we go through a life-threatening crisis ourselves and when this happens, we end up changing our stronghold beliefs.

Changing our minds to adapt to crises is to change some part or elements of our beliefs. It is perfectly normal to shift our beliefs because our beliefs are modeled on personal and communal experience.

A belief can necessarily be not true even when it has been handed down to us. In other words, a belief is not necessarily the only truth.

- **Belief is a product of the mind, faith is not**

Faith is the product of the spirit. Our mind also has a tendency to interfere with the process of faith rather than contributing it. To have confidence in the most depressing of times will require us to quiet the mind because the mind can run amok when we let it, especially when we have every negative thought clouding our mind.

Faith comes in when our beliefs run aground. Be wary that our beliefs can sway our spirit. Think of Galileo and how everyone thought the world was flat until he came around to prove that the world was indeed round. The belief that we humans have held for centuries can come and go over the course of a millennium.

- **Beliefs come and go**

But our faith is not as fickle as our belief. True faith is not a statement of our beliefs, but it is a state of being. Faith is trusting beyond all reasonable doubt and beyond all evidence that you have not been abandoned. Faith is achieved through commitment and to commit to faith is not the same thing as committing to a series of beliefs. When we are in the moment of crisis, faith tells us it doesn't matter whether its God or circumstances. To not know in the perspective of faith is to remain humble and open to learning. When faith does not fill in the cracks in a crisis, then fear will. Therefore, faith is an attitude that we create where it is the acceptance of not knowing. Unknowing is what creates faith.

Practising Creative Visualization to Encourage Self-Compassion

Creative visualization is a mental technique that harnesses our imagination to make our goals and dreams a reality. When used the right way, creative visualization has been proven to improve the lives of the people who have used it, and it also increases the success and prosperity rate of the individual. Creative visualization unleashes a power that can alter your social and living environment and circumstances, it causes beneficial events to happen, attracts positivity in work, life, relationships, and goals.

Creative visualization is not a magic potion. It uses the cognitive processes of our mind to purposely generate an array of visual mental imagery to create beneficial physiological, psychological or social effects such as increasing wealth, healing wounds to the body or alleviating psychological issues such as anxiety and sadness. This method uses the power of the mind to attract good energy and really, it is the magic potion behind every success.

Mostly, a person needs to visualize an individual event or situation or object or desire to attract it into their lives. This is a process that is similar to daydreaming. It only uses the natural process of the power of our mind to initiate positive thoughts and natural mental laws. Successful people like Oprah and Tiger Woods and Bill Gates use this technique, either consciously or unconsciously, attracting success and positive outcomes into their lives by visualizing their goals as already attained or accomplished.

- The Power of Thoughts and Creative Visualization

So how does this work and why is it so important to us?

Well, our mind is a powerful thing. With only the power of our mind, we can reach amazing success, or we can also spiral out of control. It swings both ways. Our subconscious mind accepts the ideals and thoughts that we often repeat, and when our mind accepts it, then your mindset also changes accordingly, and this influences your habits and actions. Again, a domino effect happens where you end up meeting new people or getting into situations or circumstances that lead you to your goal. Our thoughts come with a creative power that can mold our life and attract whatever we think about.

Remember the saying that goes 'mind over matter?' When we set our mind to do it, our body does what our mind tells us. Our thoughts travel from mind, body, and soul but believe it or not; it can travel from one mind to another because it is unconsciously picked up by the people you meet with every day and usually, most of the people you end up meeting are the ones who can help you achieve your goals.

You probably think and repeat certain thoughts everyday pretty often, and you probably do this consciously or unconsciously. You probably have focused your thoughts on your current situation or environment and subsequently, create and recreate the same events and circumstances regularly. While most of our lives are somewhat routine, we can always change these thoughts by visualizing different circumstances and situations, and in a way, create a different reality for you to focus on new goals and desires.

- Changing Your Reality

Honestly, though, you can change your 'reality by changing your thoughts and mental images. You aren't creating magic here; all you are doing is harnessing the natural powers and laws that inhibit each and every one of us. The thing that separates normal, average folk with wildly successful people is that the successful ones have mastered their thoughts and mental images while the rest of us are still learning or trying to cope. Changing your thoughts and attitude changes and reshapes your world.

Take for example you plan on moving into a larger apartment and instead of wallowing in self-pity such as the lack of money, do this instead- alter your thoughts and attitude and visualize yourself living in a larger apartment. It isn't difficult to do because it's exactly like daydreaming.

- Overcoming Limited Thinking

You may think daydreaming about positive things and money and success and great relationships are nothing but child's play but in fact, creative visualization can do wonders. Though that, it may be hard for different individuals to immediate alter their thoughts. Limits to this positive thinking are within us and not the power of our mind- we control it.

It might sound like its easy to change the way you think, but the truth is, it takes a lot of effort on your side to alter your thoughts at least in the immediate future. But never for a second doubt that you can't. Anything that you put your mind to work on, it can be done.

We often limit ourselves due to our beliefs and our thoughts and to the life we know. So the need to be open-minded is an integral part of positive thinking. The bigger we dare to think, the higher and great our changes, possibilities and opportunities. Limitations are created within our minds, and it is up to use to rise above all these obstacles.

Of course, it takes time to change the way we think and see things and broaden our horizons, but small demonstrations of changing our minds and the way we think will yield bigger results in due time.

- Guidelines for Creating Visualization

Concise Guidelines for Creative Visualization:

Step 1- Define your goal.

Step 2- Think, meditate and listen to your instinct, ensure that this is the goal you want to attain

Step 3- Ascertain that you only want good results from your visualization, for you and for others around you.

Step 4- Be alone at a place that you will not be disturbed. Be alone with your thoughts.

Step 5- Relax your body and your mind

Step 6- Rhythmically breathe deeply several

Step 7- Visualize your goal by giving it a clear and detailed mental image

Step 8- Add desire and feelings into this mental image- how you would feel etc

Step 9- Use all your five senses of sight, hearing, touch, taste and smell

Step 10- Visualize this at least twice a day for at least 10 minutes each time

Step 11- Keep visualizing this day after day with patience, hope and faith

Step 12- Always keep staying positive in your feelings, thoughts and words

Staying positive can be easy, it is all about training your mind. When you do feel doubts, and negative thoughts arise, replace them with positive thoughts. Also remember to keep an open mind because opportunities come in various ways so when you see it, you can take advantage of them. Every morning, or each time you conclude your visualization session, always end it with this 'Let everything happen in a favorable way for everyone and everything involved.'

Creative visualization will open doors but it takes time and whenever you feel you are in a position of advantage, take action. Do not be passive or wait for things to fall on your lap. Perhaps you've met someone who can put yours in a position of advantage to reach your goal or perhaps you've landed a job that has the possibility of enabling you to travel. All these things come into your life, and if you have an open mind, you can see the possibilities more vividly.

When you use the power of imagination for you and the people around you, always do it for good. Never try creative visualization to obtain something forcibly that belongs to others (like someone else's husband or wife or a managerial position someone else rightfully achieved but you want as well). Also, don't harm the environment.

Most visualized goals happen in a natural and gradual manner, but there can be times that can happen in a sudden and expected manner too. Be realistic with your goals, though. Don't visualize a unicorn and expect it to turn up. If money is what you desire, you know that it just will not drop from the sky. You may or may not win it in the lottery. But the chances or possibilities are higher when you go through life with a new job, or you get a promotion, or you end up making a business deal.

It is always better to think and visualize what you actually want because you do not want to attract situations that are negative, in your quest to fulfill your goals and desires.

Using Affirmations

Affirmations have helped many people make significant changes in their lives and the people around them. Do they work for everyone? Why do some people have achieved success using this technique but some people do not get anything from it?

What are Affirmations?

Affirmations are positive and direct statements that help an individual overcome self-sabotaging and negative thoughts. It helps a person visualize and believe in their goals, dreams, and abilities. In other words, you are affirming to yourself and helping yourself make positive changes to your life goals. Affirmations have the power to work because it can program a person's mind into believing a concept. The mind is known not to know the difference between what is real or fantasy. That is why when you watch a movie; you tend to empathize with the characters on the screen even though you know it's just a movie. But as soon as you leave the cinema, you are back into reality but can't help feel sorry or happy for the characters.

There are both positive and negative affirmations and some of these affirmations such as being told you are smart when you were a child or being told that you are clumsy can stick with us in both our conscious or unconscious mind. When we face failure, we tend to over-calculate the risks we are taking and work out the worst possible scenario which is usually the emotional equivalent of our parents or guardian deserting us.

We imagine an entirely dreadful scenario in our minds that we convince ourselves that trying to change isn't a good thing at all. Thus, it makes us lose out on opportunities for success and then when we actually do fail (because our mind is already convinced we'll fail anyway) the whole experience of affirmation that we give ourselves is that we are not cut out for success, or it is not in our karma to succeed, and then, we settle.

If a negative belief is firmly rooted in our subconscious mind, then it will have the ability to override any positive affirmation even when we aren't aware of it. This is one of the reasons why people do not believe in positive affirmations because it doesn't seem to be working. Their negative patterns are so high it just knocks out the sun!

So how do we add affirmations into our daily life and how can we make them prevail above our negative thinking? Here are some steps to follow:

Making Affirmations Work for You

Step 1- On a day that you are alone and not busy or distracted (if you don't have a time like this, then make one) list down all your negative qualities. Include any criticism that others have made of you and those that you have been holding onto. Remember that we all have flaws so do not judge. By acknowledging your mistakes, you can then move forward and work on your flaws, and you can make a shift in your life. When you write these down, take note to see if you are holding any grudges along the way or holding on to it. For example, do you feel tightness or dread in your heart?

Step 2- Begin to write out an affirmation on the positive aspect of your self-assessment. Use powerful statement words to beef up this assessment. Instead of saying 'I am worthy' say 'I am extremely cherished and remarkable.'

Step 3- Practice every day reading this affirmation loudly for five minutes at least three times a day in the morning, afternoon and at night before going to sleep. You can do this while shaving or putting your make up on, or when you are fixing yourself a cup of tea or if you are in the shower. At best, look in the mirror, so you look at yourself and repeat these positive statements. You can also write these affirmations in your notebook at any time you feel like it. Take note of how your writing changes over time. If we do not like something, often writing this down will encompass using smaller handwriting but if we right in big and bold letterings, we are increasing the affirmation of this. This is really a mindfulness journey to get to the agenda of positive affirmation.

Step 4- To enhance the impact, do body movements such as placing your hand on your heart when you felt uncomfortable writing out a negative criticism of yourself in Step 1. As you work on reprogramming your mind to alter it from the concept of affirmation to a real and definite personification of the quality that you see.

Step 5- Get someone to help you repeat your affirmations. This can be a friend or a gym coach or just about anyone that you feel safe with. For example, if they are saying that you are cherished and remarkable, and then connect this statement with your situations such as 'excellent colleague' or 'good fathering.' If you are not comfortable with doing this with someone, then look at your reflection in the mirror and reinforce your positive message.

Affirmations can be an incredibly powerful tool that can help you change your state of mind, alleviate your mood and more importantly, ingrain the changes your desire into your life. But for all of this to happen, you first need to identify the negative and the work on getting rid of them in your life.

Examples of Positive Affirmation

Here are some examples of positive affirmations that you can use to relate to the various areas of your development:

- I know, accept and am true to myself
- I believe in myself and have confidence in my decisions
- I eat a balanced diet, exercise regularly and get plenty of rest
- I always learn from my mistakes
- I know I am capable of anything and can accomplish anything I set my mind to
- I have flaws and I am not perfect but that's ok because I am human
- I never, ever give up
- I can adapt and accept what I have no control over
- I make the best of every situation
- I always look at the bright side of life
- I enjoy life to the fullest
- I stand up for what I believe in, my morals and my values
- I treat others with respect and recognize their individuality
- I can make a difference
- I can practice understanding, patience and compassions
- I am always up to learn new things and be open-minded
- I live in the moment and learn from my past and prepare for my future

These are just some of the positive affirmations that you can use to be optimistic and pursue a fulfilling and happy mindset. Have fun in creating your own affirmations or tailor the above to suit your needs and situation. Most of the affirmations above can be used daily to uplift, inspire and motivate you and those around you.

Mindfulness Meditation for Self-Compassion

Have you thought about meditation or have you done meditation before? Meditation does wonders to your body, mind and soul. When it comes to practising self-compassion, mindful meditation helps you incorporate this into your daily life more frequently. Keep in mind that mindful meditation isn't only helpful for self-compassion but it also helps us deal with the negativity that we face when we want to practice self-compassion.

Exercise 1 – Mindful Breathing

Breathing is an essential part of the meditative experience, so it is only natural that we should

exercise this too. Whenever you meditate, you're breathing mindfully when you focus on each purposeful breath that goes in and out of your body. Mindful breathing doesn't just have to happen when you're meditating, it can be done anywhere and at any time whether you're sitting, standing or just walking about. Make it a habit to breathe mindfully and you'll find it much easier to do so during your meditation sessions.

1. Start by bringing your attention and focus to your breathing.
2. Breathe in slowly for approximately 3 seconds, and then release that breathe slowly, counting to 3 seconds again.
3. During this exercise, you should focus and be thinking of nothing else except your breathing. Do not think about the tasks you need to do, or a meeting that is coming up at work.

Think about nothing but your breathing in and out, counting the seconds as you do.

4. Concentrate on the air that is filling your lungs as you breathe in, the way it makes your body feel, and when you release your breathe, imagine all the stress and the tension leaving your body as you do.

You can do this for 1-2 minutes at a time throughout the day, several times a day and you're already on your way towards improving each meditation session when you get better at learning to control your breathing.

Exercise 2 – Awareness

When you meditate, you learn to become more aware of your body, your mind and your thoughts, aware of what is happening all around you when your eyes are closed because your other senses become heightened when your eyes are shut. Being mindfully aware helps you sharpen your focus and remain alert to not just your surroundings, but your thoughts as well. For example, if you were mindfully aware about your thoughts, you will have better control when it comes to keeping any negative thought or emotion at bay.

Exercising your awareness throughout the day will help sharpen your alertness towards everything around you. Not just around you, but within you too. Beginners often find focusing on awareness to be a struggle in the beginning, because its so easy to let our thoughts drift and get distracted by everything else. Training yourself to be more aware will help you better connect your mind and body during your meditation sessions, so it's a good idea to practice these throughout the day to help you sharpen your focus and cultivate a heightened sense of awareness.

1. Start by choosing an activity or an object to focus on. Pick something that you would normally do without thinking twice about it, like opening the door or getting dressed in the morning for example.

2. Once you've got your object or activity, start to really, actively pay attention to what you're doing. If you're opening the door, concentrate on it. Reach for the doorknob and be aware of how it feels in your hand, and the motion of pulling the door towards you or away from you. Stop and appreciate how lucky you are to be healthy and fit enough to walk out your front door with a destination and a purpose in mind.

3. When you're getting dressed in the morning, focus and be aware of what you're doing instead of just going through the motions. Concentrate on how the fabric of your clothes feel in your hand, and even stop to appreciate how fortunate you are to be able to have a selection of clothes to choose from as you go through your closet looking for something to wear.

4. Before you eat, be aware of the food that is in front of you, how good it smells, the shapes, the colors. As you take each bite and begin to chew, be aware of how the food tastes and you take each bite with purpose.

Eventually, being mindfully aware is something that will come much easier, and the more you practice the easier you will find it is to concentrate on what you're doing or thinking without becoming easily distracted by other thoughts around you.

Exercise 3 – Mental Focus

Successful meditation involves being able to concentrate and not let your thoughts get easily distracted, which means you're going to need to work on improving your focus. Exercises to improve your focus are simple enough, here's what you can do:

1. Pick an object to focus on and place it in front of you.
2. When you're ready, set a timer and start to focus on the object and nothing else.
3. Concentrate on that object and keep staring at it for as long as you can.
4. When your mind begins to wander, stop and make a note of how long you managed to concentrate on that object before your mind started to drift.
5. Next round, do the same thing but try to go for a longer time this time around, aiming to beat your previous record.

Gradually, you should be able to focus on the object in front of you for longer periods of time before you find yourself getting distracted. The longer you can focus on the object, the better your focusing abilities will become.

Conclusion

I want to first and foremost thank you for reading this book in its entirety. I hope that the expertise I have gained over the years along with sprinkling my personal experiences with anxiety has helped you to gain a new perspective as well as a new lease on life.

Anxiety is something that every single person must face, even when they least expect it. You can either continue to give it the power to wreak havoc on your everyday life, or you can choose to do your best to lessen or even eliminate it completely with the techniques and strategies you have just learned from the previous chapters.

My hope is that by educating even just a few people on the power of taking back control of your life with self-awareness, positive thinking, and re-engineering the mind, that our world can become a better place, one healed mind at a time.

Self-Compassion takes practice no doubt. One of the first few things you can do is to change the way you perceive self-compassion- by dispelling the myths and creating a positive perception towards self-love. Through the power of affirmations, creative visualization as well as changing your ideas of faith and believe, you can definitely start being more mindful of who you are what, and not based on your achievements and failures.

Knowing the myths of self-compassion is definitely one of the first things you should understand if you are really serious about wanting to be self-compassionate. This is only because whenever you feel like you are going to the downward spiral of thinking negative thoughts, you can always remember what self-compassion is and what self-compassion is not.

Self-compassion is a a good thing- keep this in mind so work on it because it does make you a better person.

CPSIA information can be obtained
at www.ICGtesting.com
Printed in the USA
BVHW081501021220
594682BV00002B/696